I0836960

Naked In Wonderland

Volume Three

CEArts Press

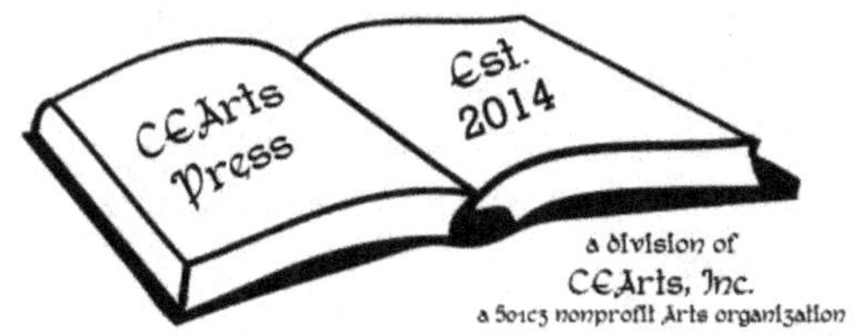

First Printing: August 2020

Cover design and original artwork:
Alys Caviness-Gober
Project design, formatting, and layout:
Alys Caviness-Gober
Editor:
Alys Caviness-Gober

ISBN: 978-0-9998858-4-0

Community • Education • Arts Press
a division of *Community • Education • Arts, Inc.*
Noblesville, IN 46060
https://CEArts.org

Ordering Information:
Special discounts are available on quantity purchases by corporations, associations, educators, and others.
Please contact Alys at info@cearts.org for details.
U.S. trade bookstores and wholesalers: please contact Alys at info@cearts.org for details.

dedicated to my family

Introduction

There's no *Introduction* in my two prior volumes of my poetry and artwork collection series, *Naked In Wonderland.* The collections lay out my poetry in chronological order, with some of my original artwork inserted here and there. Putting my poems in chronological order makes it easy to see if or how my writing evolved over time. The volumes always contain some pieces that I wish to rework further ~ but, I accept that they are done. I've been working on *Volume Three* for over six years.
I can't quite believe it's been that long.

One reason this collection has taken me so long to put together is that about six years ago, I created an all-volunteer 501(c)(3) nonprofit arts organization. Managing it, fundraising for it, and creating and organizing and hosting its events became pretty much *almost* all I was doing creatively for the past six years. Recently, due to the global pandemic, my nonprofit arts organization has become 100% virtual, offering remote and online arts events and opportunities to creatives of all kinds. It still takes up a lot of my time, but I love being able to offer a variety of artistic opportunities to other creatives. We're all in this world together, and I believe in supporting and encouraging other creatives.

There are other reasons this volume's taken so long for me to finish. My father passed away in 2014 and my mother passed in 2017. A lot of my poetry reflect those losses, which took away so much of the creative and happy part of my heart and soul. I know this volume is colored by the loss of my parents; I'm pretty sure the rest of my creative life will continue to be haunted (both lovingly and poignantly) by them. So much of this book includes processing my grieving for my parents and that's why I decided to include an *Introduction.* All of us face loss; I hope you find comfort and sympathy in some of my poems.

So much of *myself* returned to me when our first grandchild was born in March of 2019; he's my Little Paly, forever. From the time he was born through mid-March 2020, I took care of him Mondays through Fridays, from 7:00AM to about 5:00PM, while his parents worked. Believe me, I ***happily*** gave up a lot of my artsy time to care for him.

As this volume goes to print in August of 2020, I now see my little grandson remotely every day at his dinnertime, onscreen in video chats, because everything changed with COVID-19. I'm living in isolation, because I'm in the most at-risk group, with many pre-existing health issues. It's heartbreaking to not be able to share in the lives of my loved ones in person. My writings and artwork post-March 2020 are forthcoming in *Volume Four* of my collections series. I hope to meet you someday in person, at a book fair or author's event. In the meantime, as I watch the world go by from my window, stay safe and stay strong.

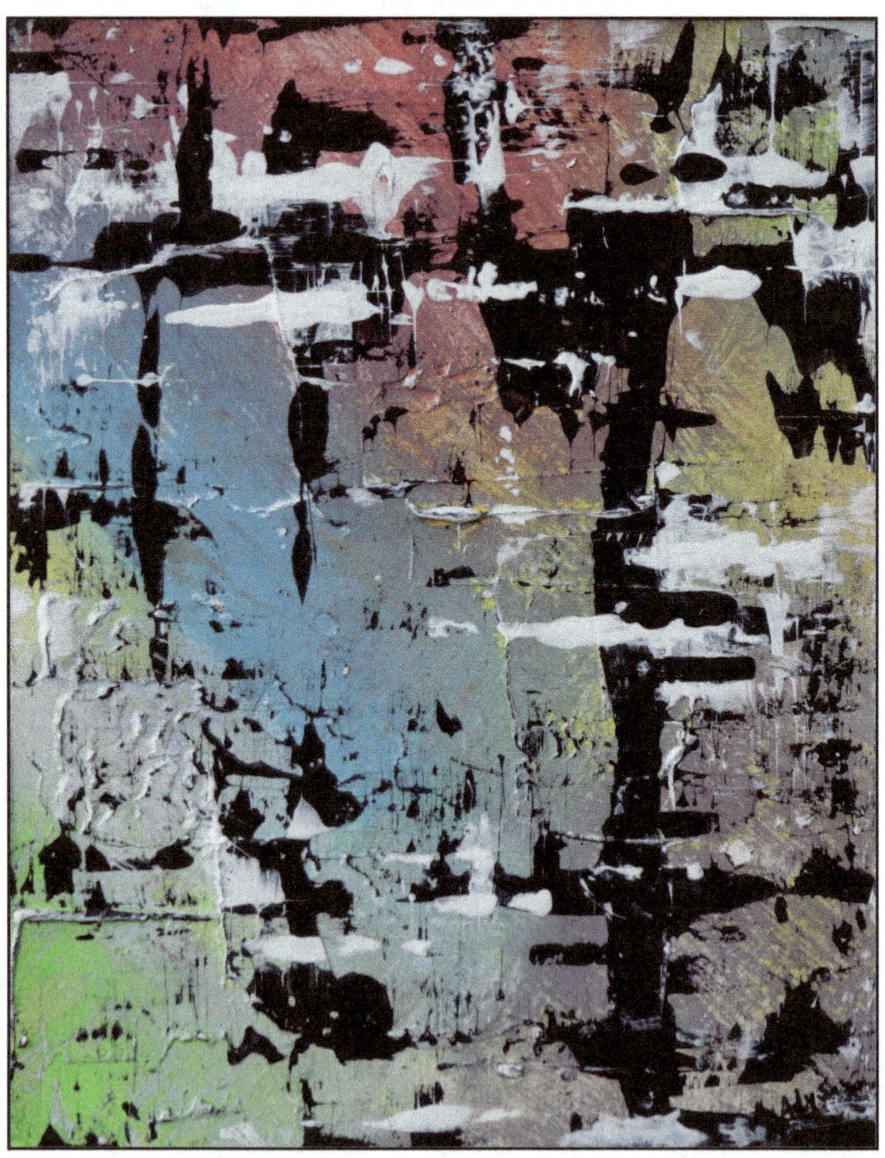

Table of Contents

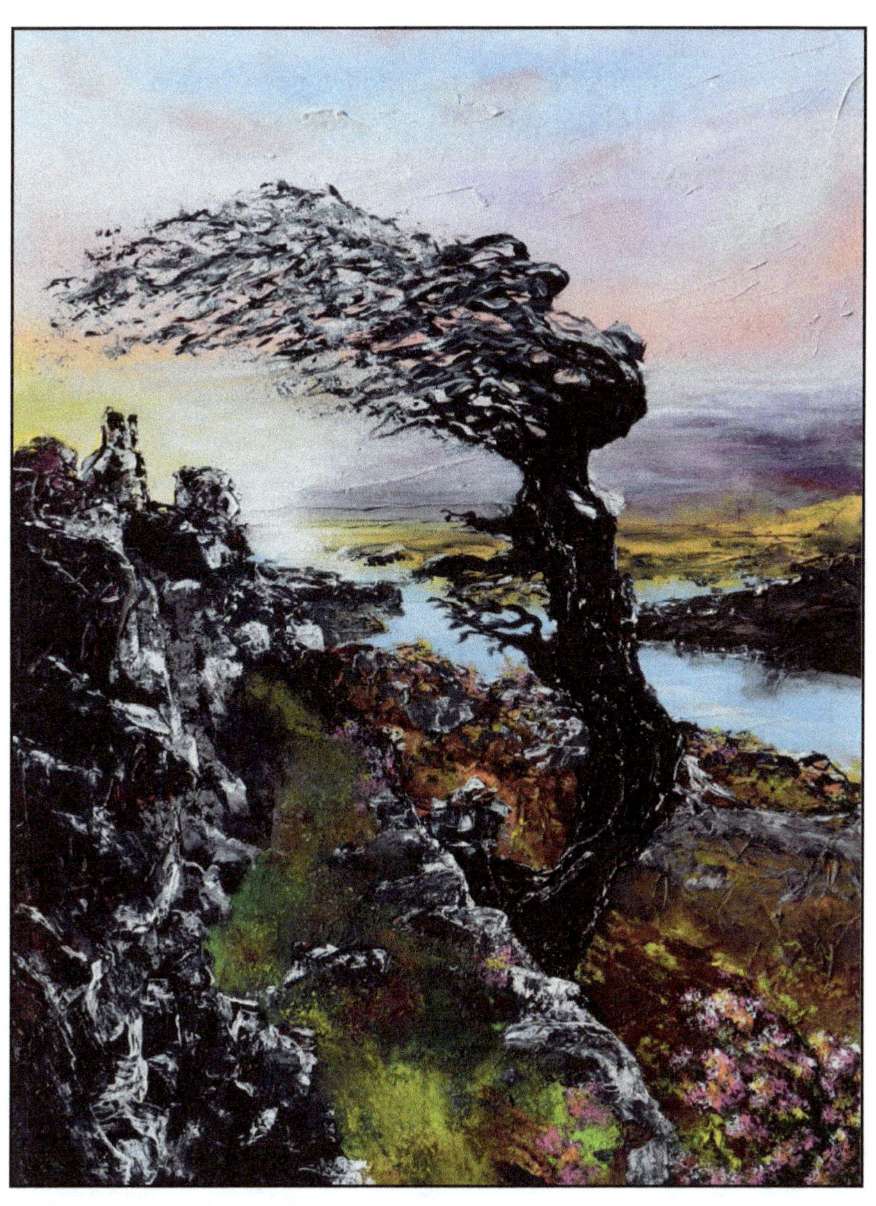

Force Of Nature

She was warned
by the winds that beat her.
She was warned
by the sun that cracked her.

She was warned
by the rains that eroded her.
She was given an explanation
by the tempestuous gods above her.

Nevertheless,
she persisted
as a force of nature,
uncontrolled.

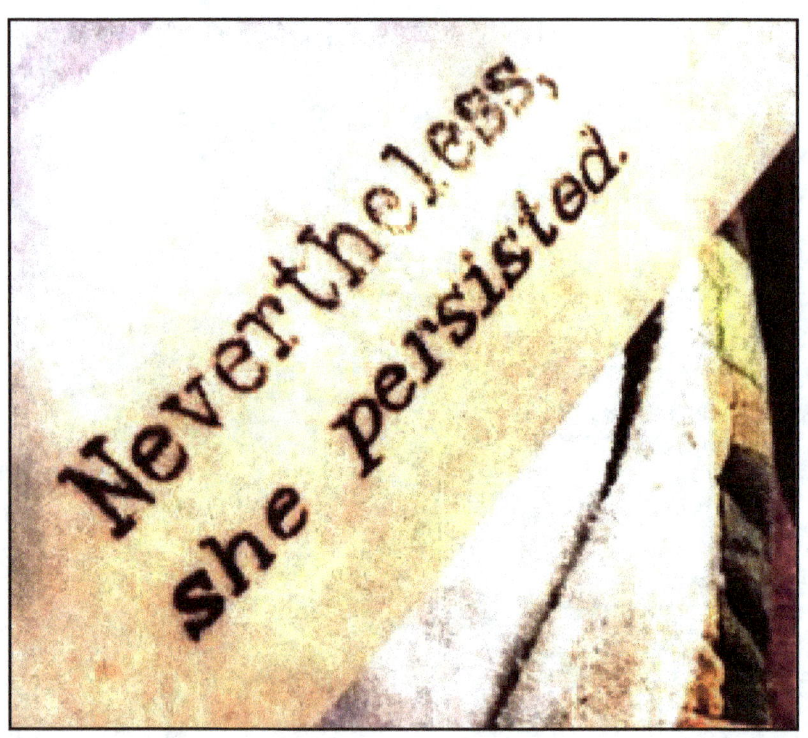

Apropos Of Nothing

apropos of nothing
I call your name in silence
casting wide a dark desire
come luminous into my dreams
apropos of nothing
I touch the burning fence

searing with earthquake's fire
come luminous into my dreams

apropos of nothing
in a fatal stolen sense
collapsing now together
come luminous into my dreams

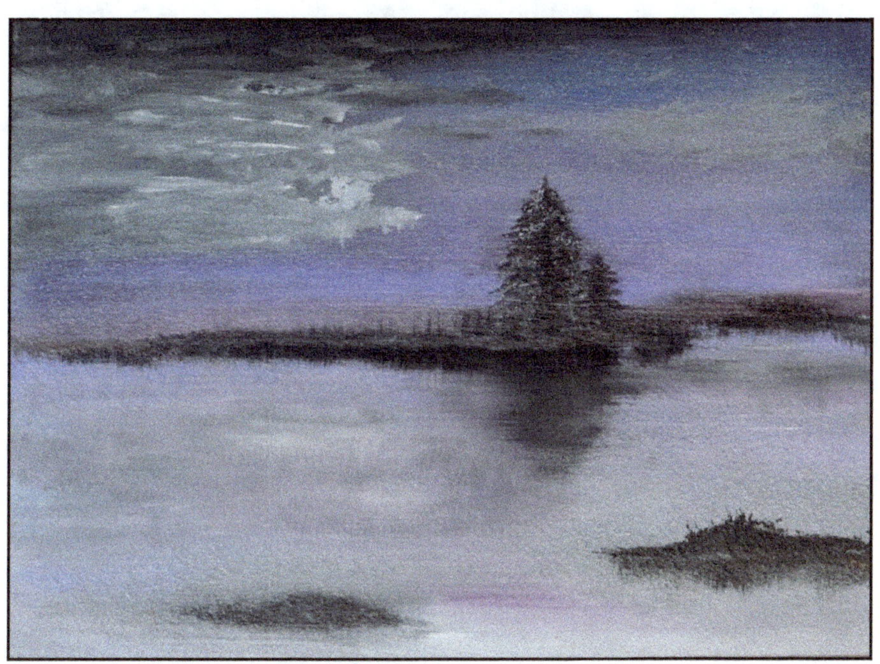

Slow Jazz

like a dream bending
a river flowing
night descending
and shadows lingering
he plays slow jazz
for me

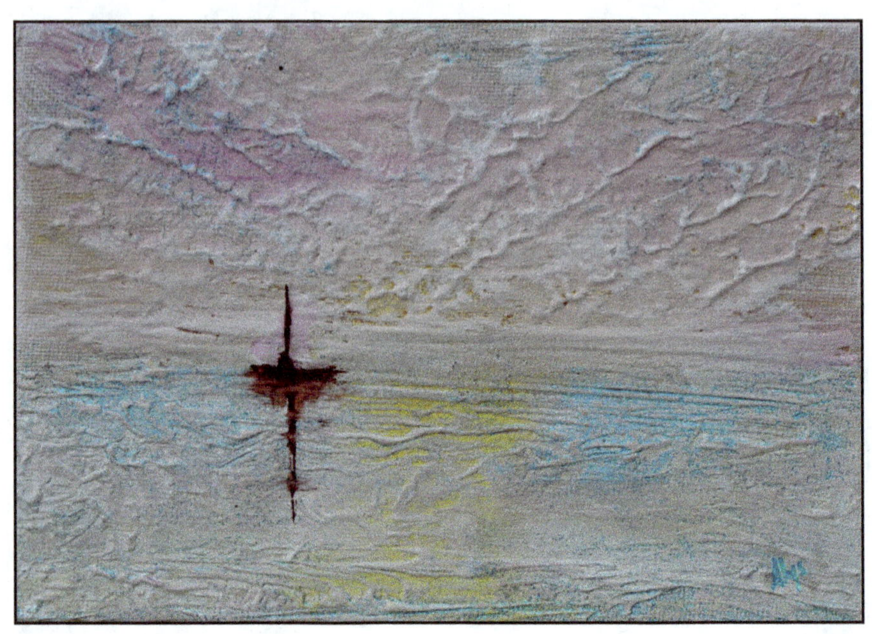

Monsters

the beat of the drum
goes *thrum-thrum-thrum*;
grinning and spinning
you feel them winning
every heart in the room
with a flick of their tongues
over red lips and pink gums,
with a chomp and a grind
and a sparkalling shine
you're drawn right on in
by Dr. Frankenfurter's gleam,
his alien beam
of fatherly pride
erupts from inside,
because she's just like him,
she barks, triumphant
"Show me your TEETH!"
~ and the monsters go wild ~

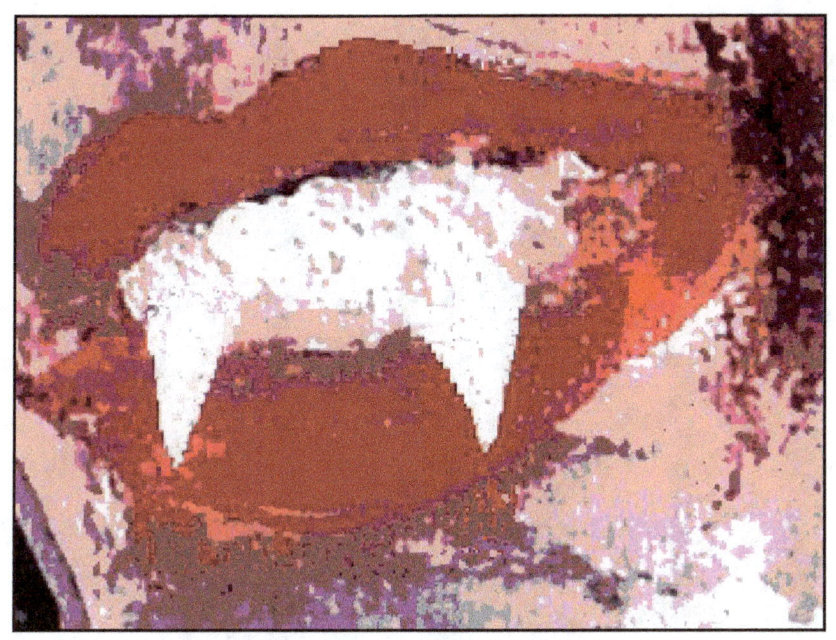

Like Bones

for a mother, they change everything,
and turn her baby into a child
~ cutting through ~
~ solid food ~
like bones, they tell a story;

for a lover, they light up any room
and turn a simple smile
into an open heart
~ a soul bared ~
~ cracked wide ~
like bones, they tell a story;
for an archaeologist, they last the longest
and turn the ancient past
into today
~ what they ate ~
~ why they died ~
like bones, they tell a story

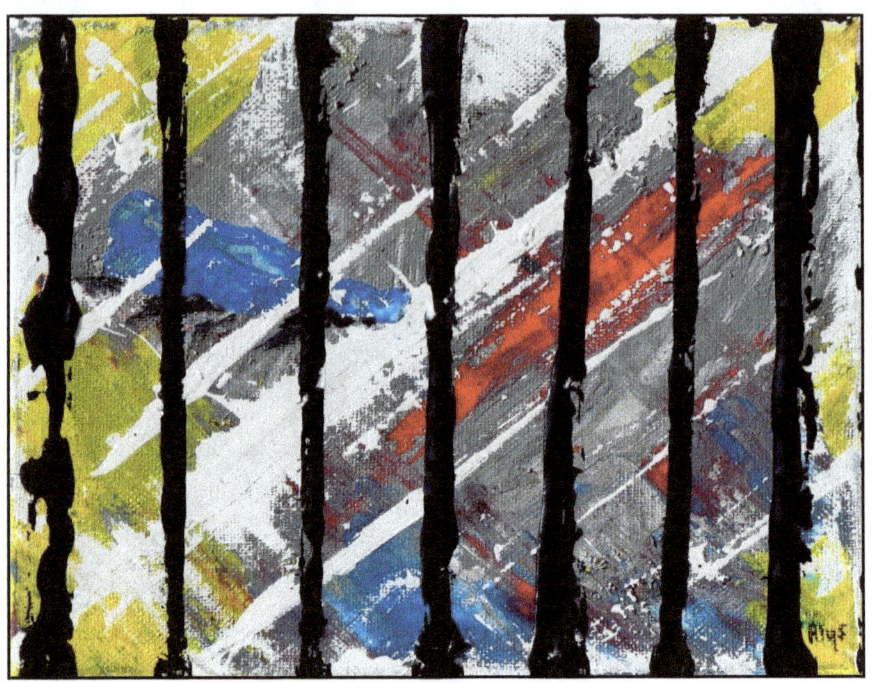

Devastation

Quench this thirst unyielding,
deny my sight this darkness;
come inside and play
like music soothes
and lovers tease.

Behind shuttered eyelids,
behind his prison bars,
a bottle falls.

Recent Convert

We trudge
uphill most of the time
towards a brighter day
and perhaps peace of mind
and you take my hand

because you *Believe*
and want to lead me
to *The Light*.

My spirit feels
splintered
and defiant
because some days
your Religion
blocks the sun
from me
and there is only the Darkness
of your Blind Faith
but then
the beauty of your colors
converts me.

On The Red Bridge

someday when you lay down
the weight of our world
and your body is free of pain
and your soul is free of worry
and your eyes become stars

then come find me
on the Red Bridge
where I shall be waiting
and I shall be watching for you

then take my hand
in yours once more
and we'll be young again
as we walk across the Red Bridge
together

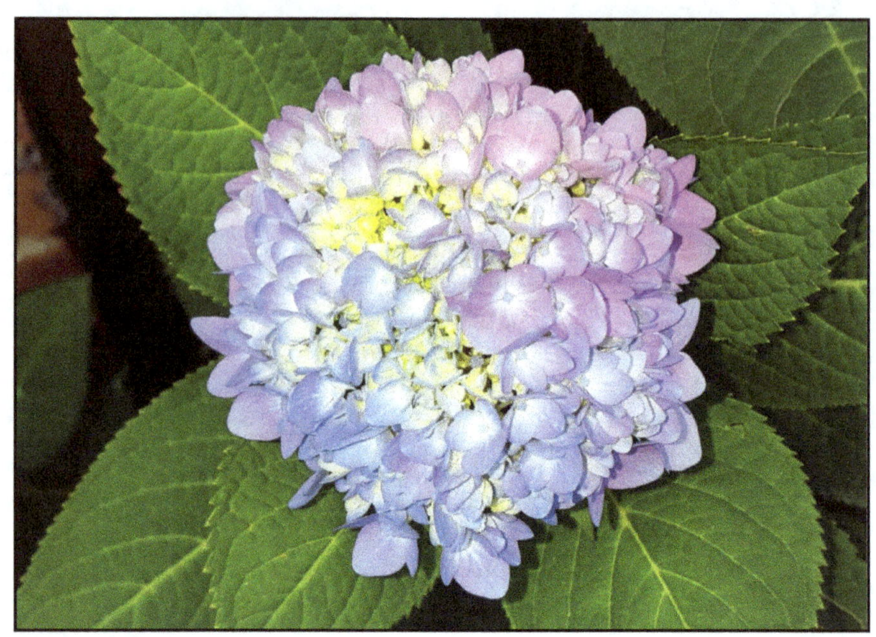

Waves

out in the distance
you can see the horizon
where the line between heaven and earth
blurs softly into the ocean;
a little frightening,
yet it beckons,
and you cannot resist ~
stepping from the rolling sands
into the churning surf
feeling the water eat your ankles
then caress your legs
and you hop and float
in its embrace just a little
as your waist then chest
dip into the sea
while your eye is fixed upon that line
softly gently luring you further
until the waves take you away

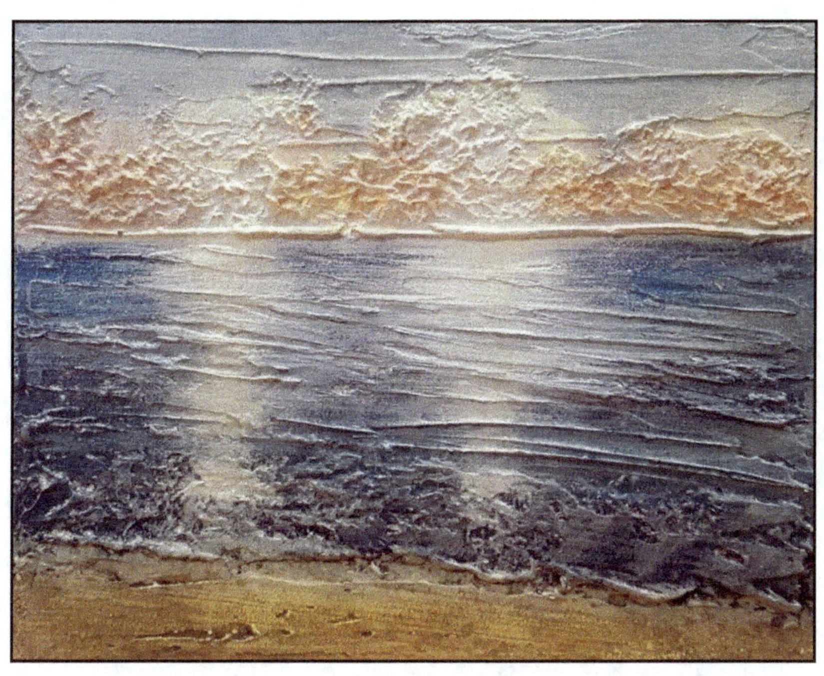

Half Asleep

it comes unbidden
touching me
like a soft sea mist
like a warming ray of sunlight
like the tickling caress
of a lick of the waves

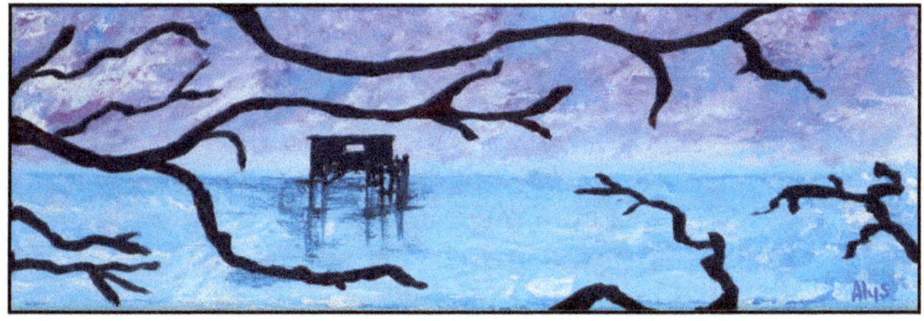

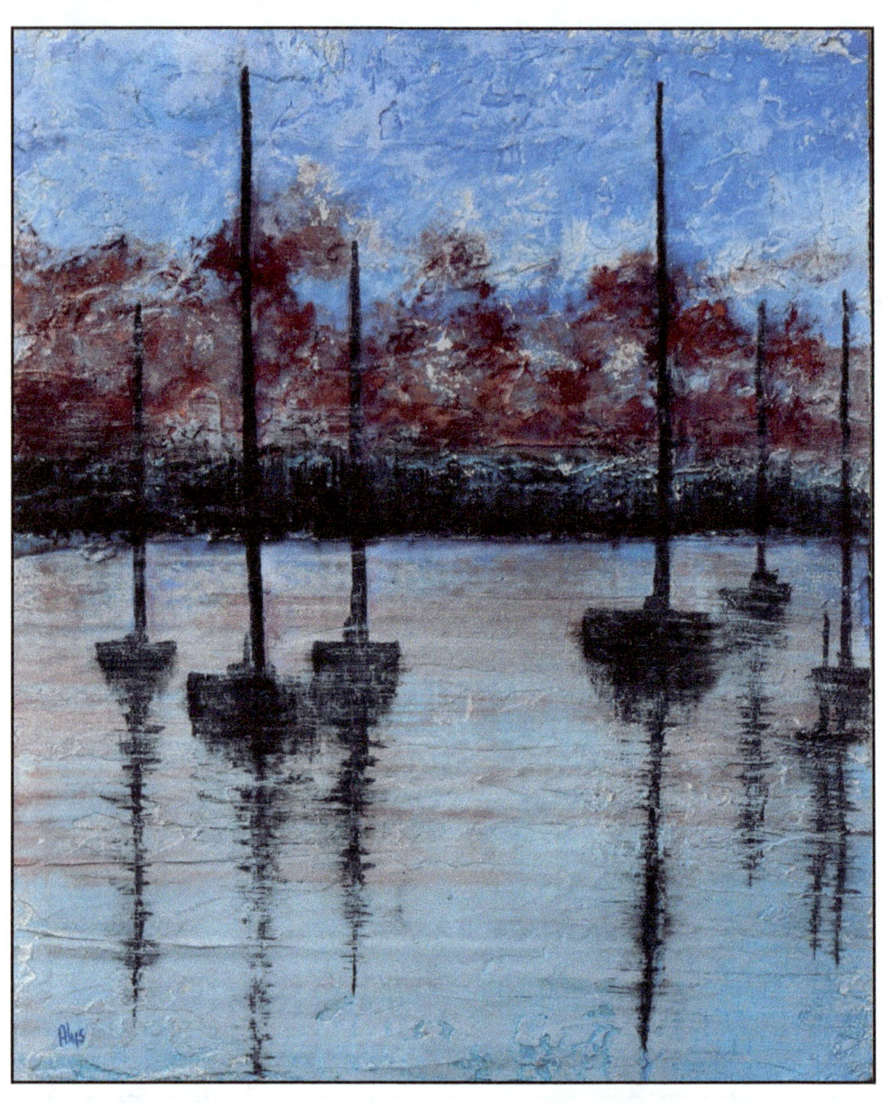

A Red Storm

looking back
at cool blues and grays
always there curving around
carrying and lifting over and through
grief and pain always there
your cool blues and grays

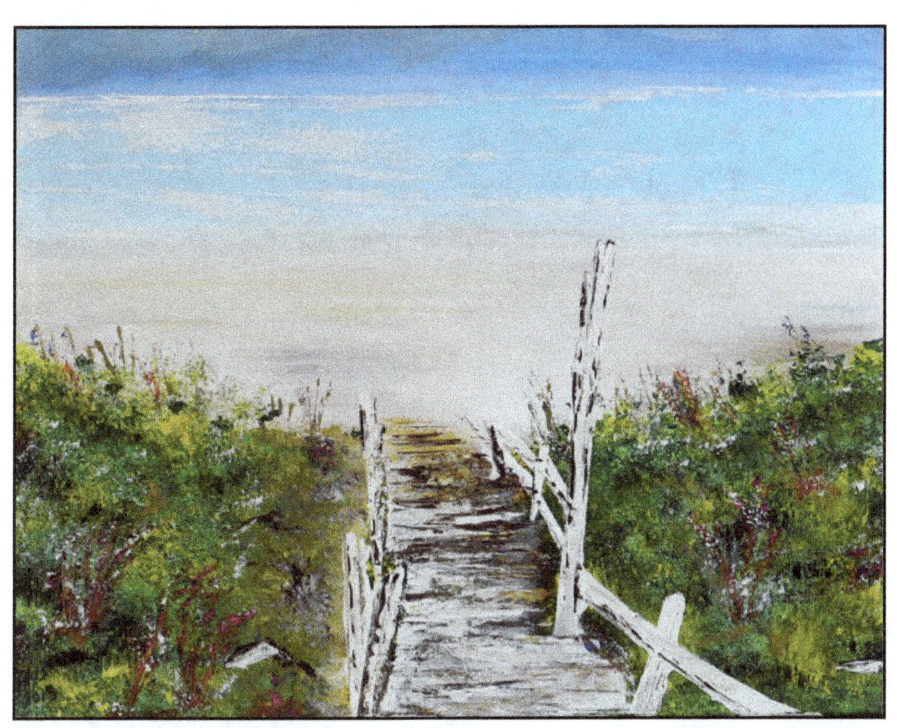

Untitled

The early days of Spring bring a longing
and a dream
of going to the beach,
where in the cutting sand
a sharp desire is met,
where salt-winds caress me like a favored lover,
where the ocean meets the sky
and eternity is mine ~
I dream then I awake
in this landlocked dawn,
yet almost I can feel
that sharp white sand
against my warming skin,
and almost I can see
that sweet blue lover's sky
kiss the salty singing sea.

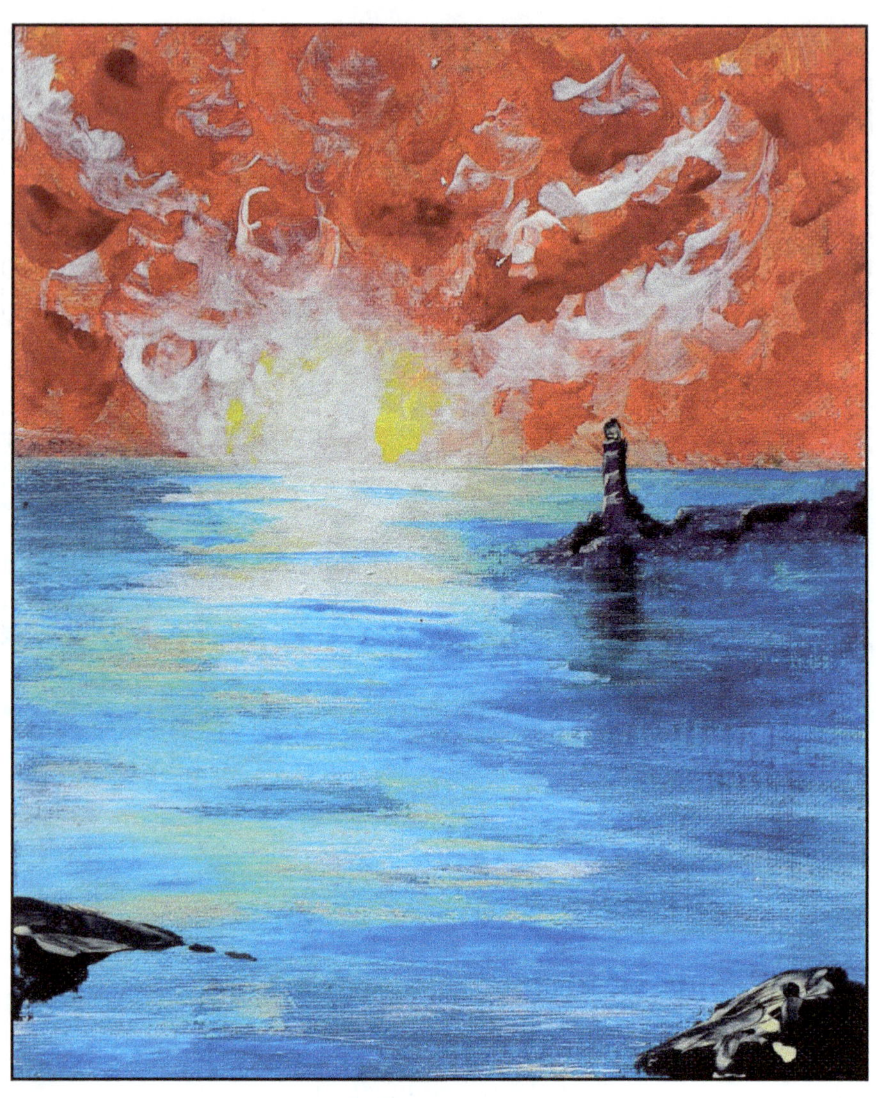

Lighthouse

somewhere sunset gleams
upon windswept weathered stone
a sea gull calls out

July Power Outage

No power
4over an hour
makes me sour.

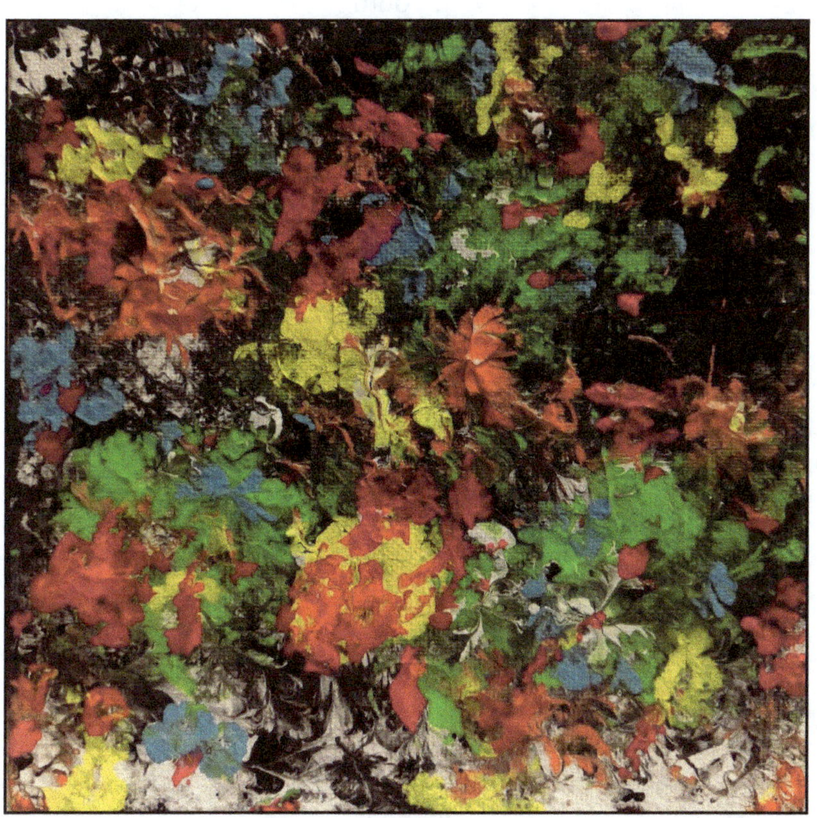

Victory

for my great-Uncle Boris,
WWII Concentration Camp Survivor,
and for my children

even faded by decades,
the blue tattoo still screams,
(not like you see in movies,
a character's temporary prop)

documenting survival,
remembering
the Truth,

a gentle and quiet man,
grown old and worn
in youth

ever haunted by the dead
after his gift of
freedom,

you are his tribute to them,
his Victory
eternal

Parallel Lives

Running
on familiar roads,
we saw
the same skies
and seas,
the sun shone
upon us
with equal heat,

and we breathed in
and out
the same air,
we spoke to people
and heard them
answer back,

we went on together side by side,
but always
you saw more
than a few dark clouds
scuttling
across the colors
that ribboned through

the world,
and
always
you saw prison bars
and lines in the sand
and rough hard edges
and knives
sharply cutting;

we lived parallel lives
differently.

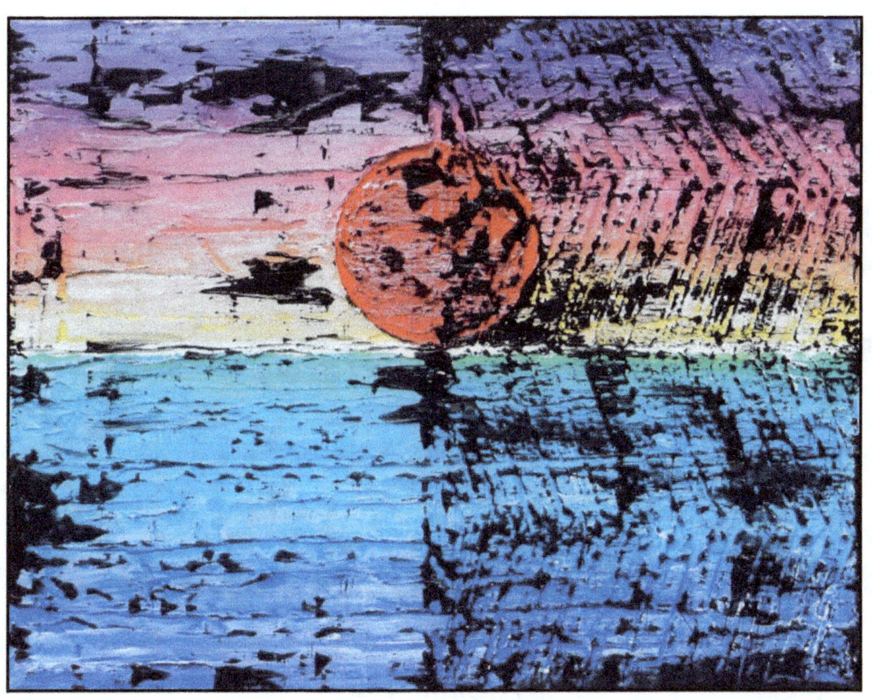

Riding Out The Storm

soft raindrops fall
from amethyst clouds
misty and sweet
they slowly build

harder and faster
until a sheet of water
cascades and floods
like a waterfall
or a solid screen

shielding everything
except the birds
who hide under amber leaves
riding out the storm

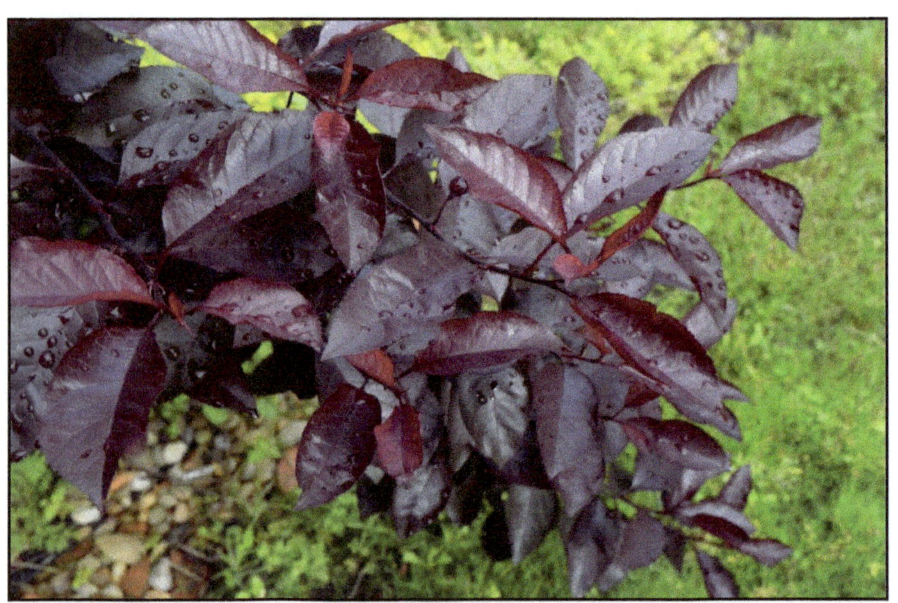

Washing Day

Prayers rise,
lifting sins confessed.

O, those quiet moments
with The Divine,

when peace descends
like a soft Spring rain

washing away
Winter's debris.

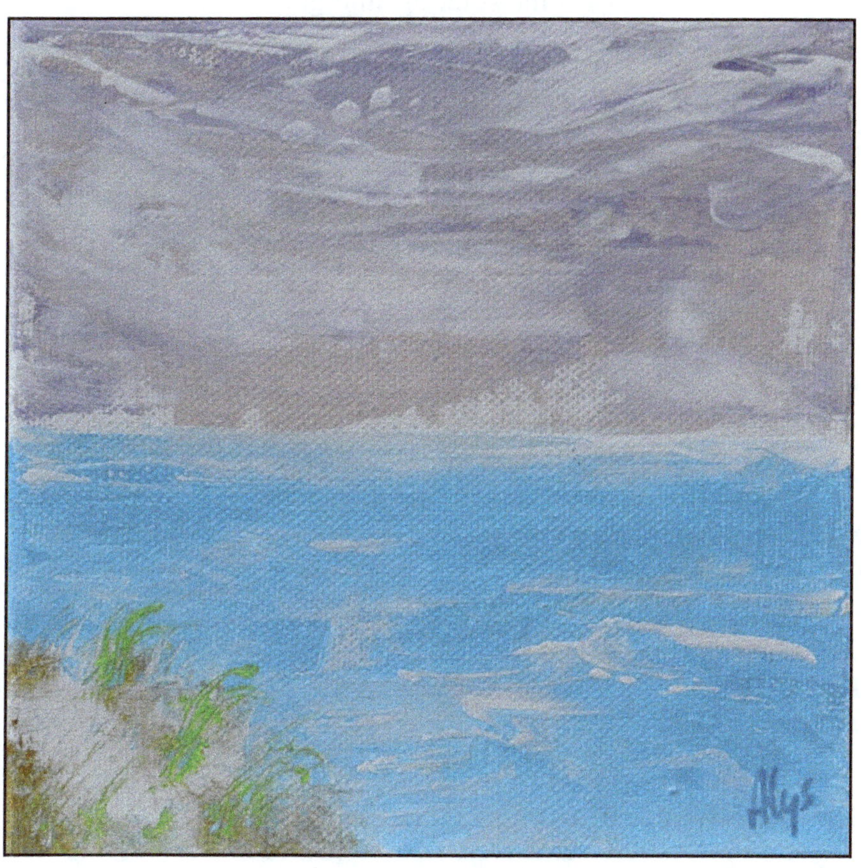

At Moor

We lay upon her deck
bathed wet in sweat and moonlight
and our boat rocked beneath us
on the wild waves we'd made
mirroring a madness of clouds
crashing together above us;

we lay upon her deck
as your breath mingled mine

and she moved more gently now
with sweet caution and delight
a soft sigh like the last white rays
of the slinking sunlight;

we lay upon her deck
pretending to be Kate and Bogey
and she was our own *African Queen*
"but Chah-lee," I said,
"we cahn't just go 'round and 'round,
we cahn't just go 'round and 'round"
and your laughter echoed to Heaven;

we lay upon her deck
entwined and outstretched together
and our boat rocked beneath us
as ripples to and from the darkened shore
slapped wetly upon her sides
and we slept, at moor.

Sometimes

I hear the Witching Hour approach
saturated with dark reproach

when yesterday's undaunted path
became Destiny's rigid wrath;

sometimes I yearn to tread once more
my footsteps backwards through that door,

sometimes I yearn once more to see
a path unspoken awaiting me.

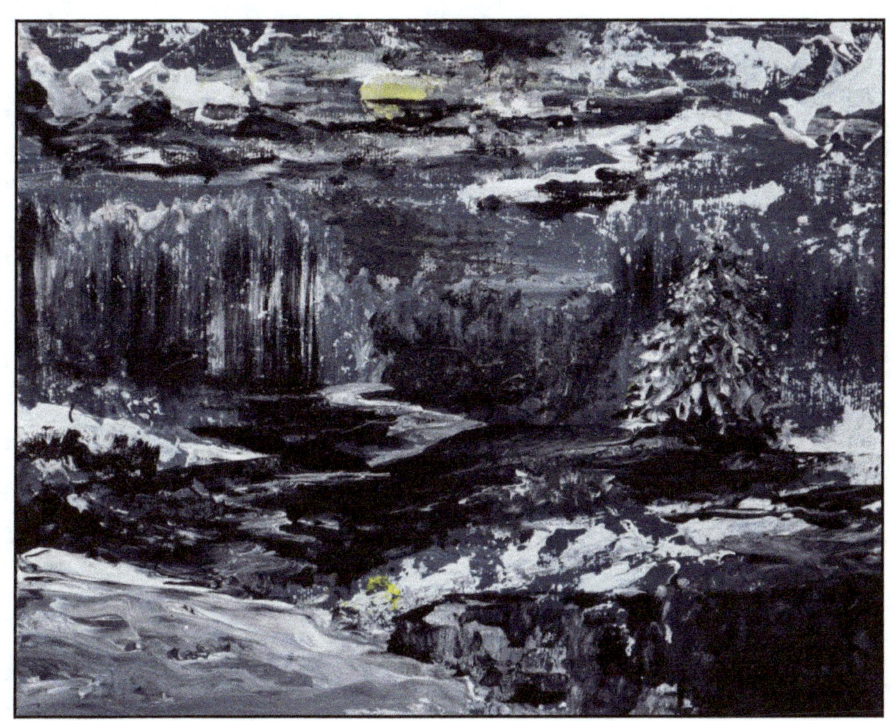

Shadows

In a flash,
I turn,
but a flash is too slow
and it's too late;
there's nothing left
but shadows.

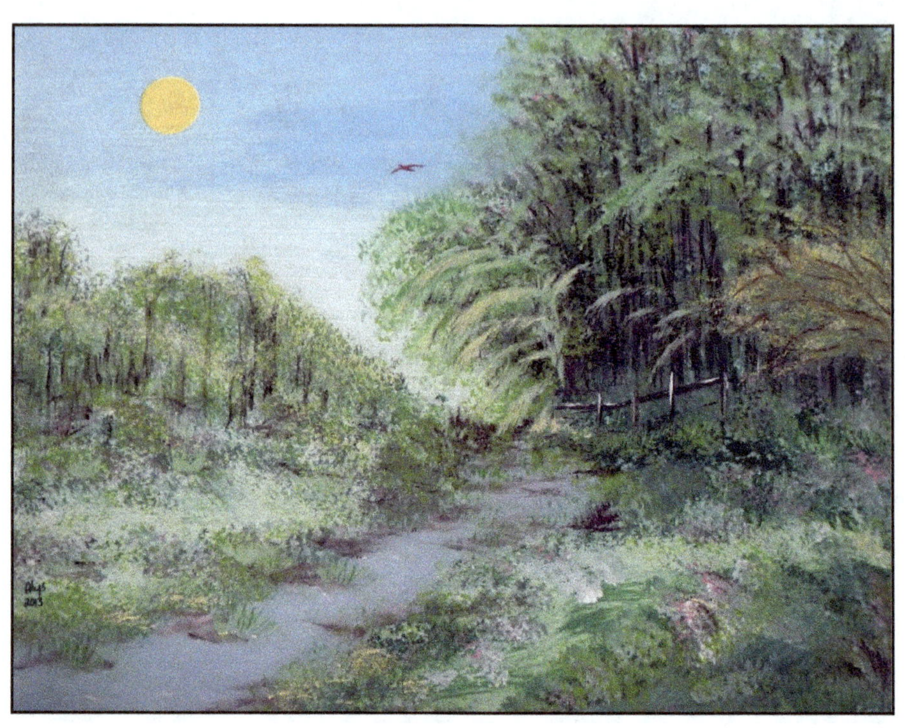

The Longest Week

Looking into your eyes,
I saw you leave before the ambulance came,
but she wasn't ready to let you go;
it was a long week,
in the ICU.

We were all there,
loving you ~ our Dad, their Grandpa ~
but you'd been hers all through forever;
it was a long week,
watching her hope die.

Everyone was nice,
they kept you safe in that glass-walled room
of tubes and machines and despair;
it was a long week,
and still I hear those machines.

I turned fifty-one years old
by your hospital bed, holding your hand
and crying, trying to find words;
it was a long week,
letting you go.

There was no beauty there for you
or for us, there was only sadness
and loss and a novel harsh reality;
it was a long week,
in a gruesome system.

If only you had been
a beloved dog or cat or even a horse,
we could have spared you
the longest week.

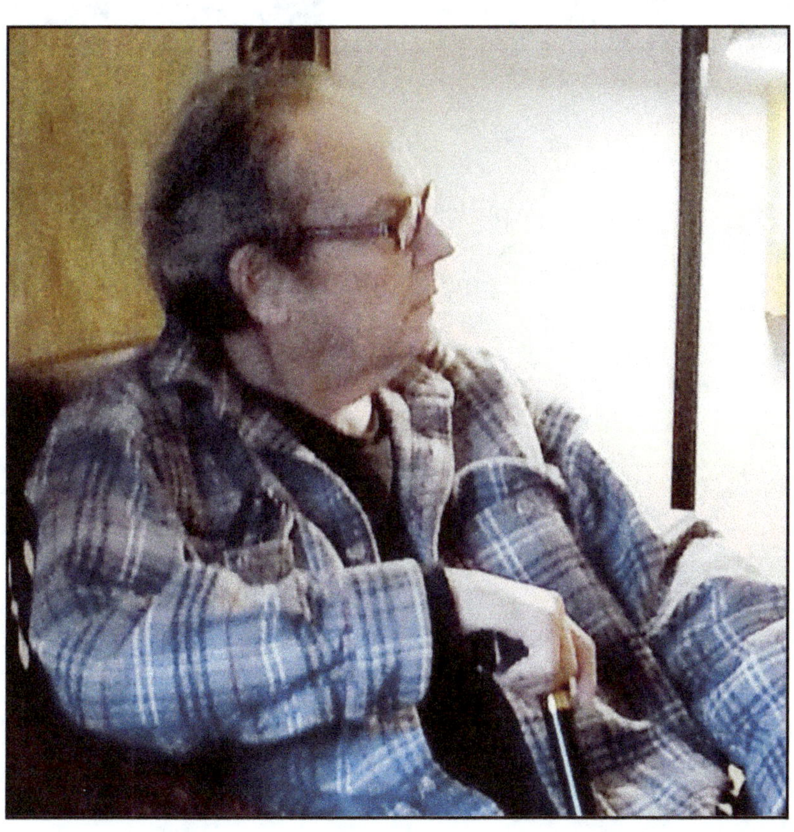

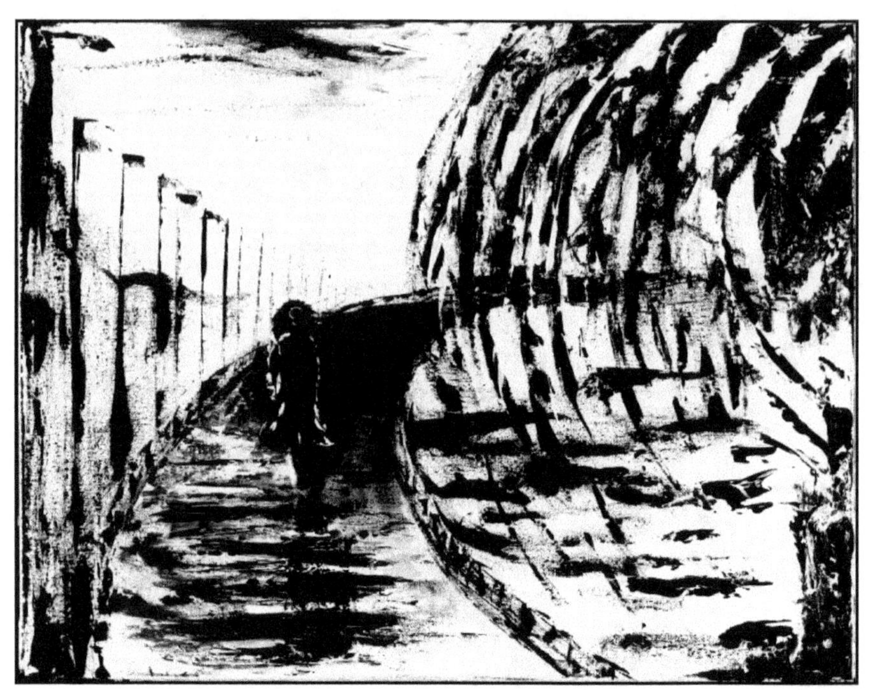

June

pitiless clouds fly
ferocious summer begins
weeping ghost wanders

Waiting

Nothing stopped.
Everything stopped.
I'm waiting.

Somewhere in between
nothing and everything,
I'm waiting.

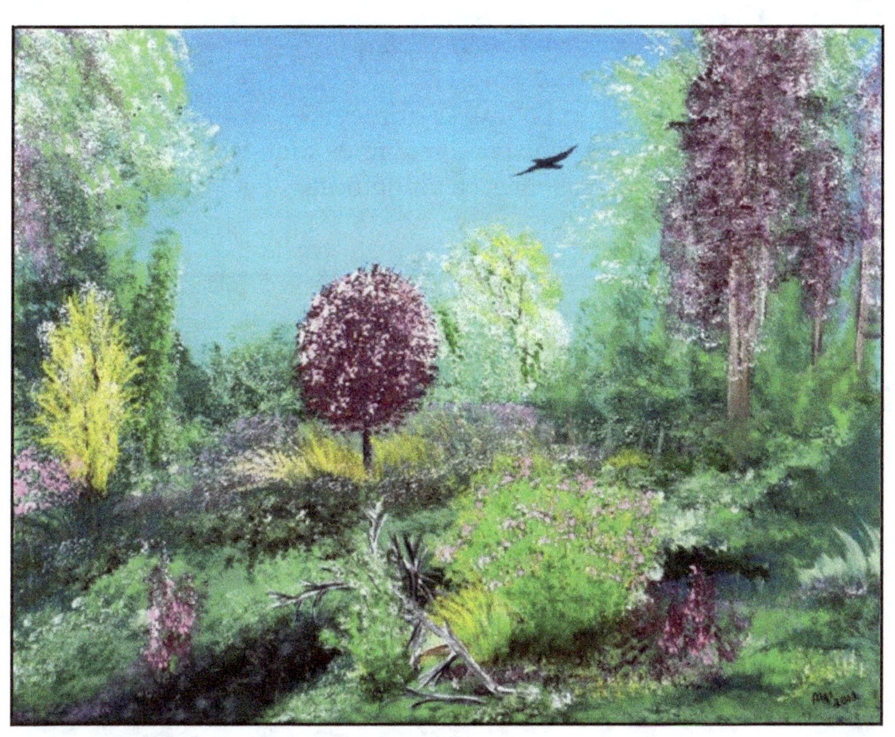

Indiana Spring Afternoon By The Creek

Aloft, bright sapphire and topaz skies
shine freshly down and through peridot and citrine
sprinkled with amethyst and tourmaline;
Indiana's born again.

Home

When the sea grass whispers my name through leeward winds,
and the indigo stained sky shines down into caressing waves,
and the great-tailed grackle steps so lightly
across hot diamond sands,
then, yes, and only then
will I again breath in
the sweet southern salty air
of home.

Unparalleled

a yellow sky dreams
above whispered summer sounds
his eyes catching mine

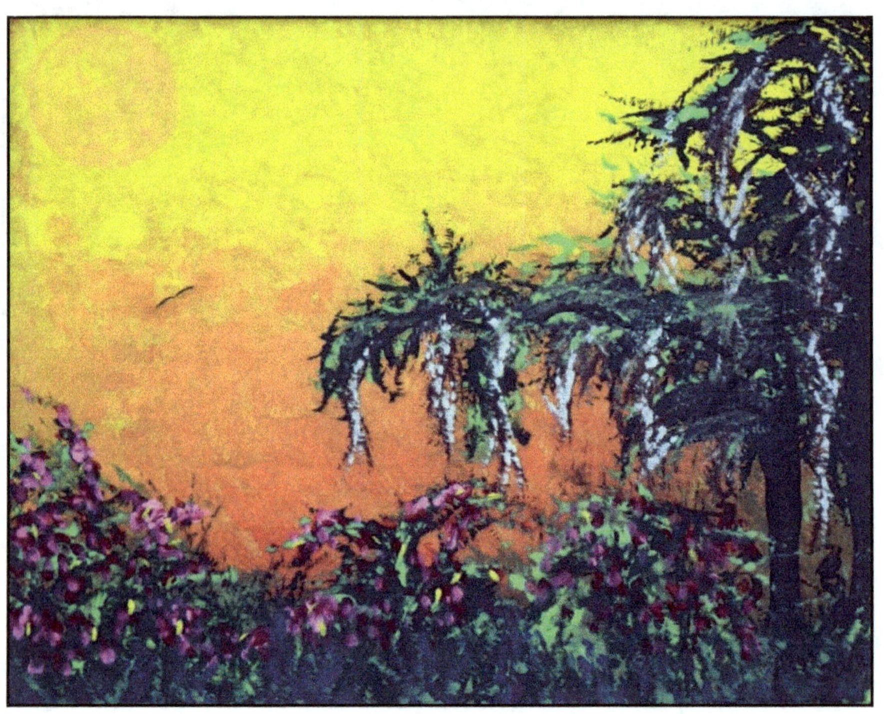

The Pastel Scarf

She saved her money,
pin money, pocket money,
they called it,
now, what I'd call spare change,
pennies, nickels, and dimes,
quarters and the occasional
one dollar bill,
all saved over a long gray Winter,
stashed in that old candy tin,
waiting patiently
to purchase a small luxury

to welcome Spring;
something bright
to wear for Easter,
something worth every penny.

She found it, the perfect scarf,
at Meyer & Franks ladies' counter,
swirling softly
among the crisp white gloves
and thick leather handbags,
its raggedly abstract pastel colors
dancing on the translucent white silk
looked to her like flowers and butterflies,
and the drifting ends made her smile
as she whirled it around her crown
of strawberry hair;
it was worth every penny.

She gave it to her grownup daughter,
on a warm Summer birthday,
a hand-me-down gift,
a remembrance of child's play ~
when her daughter traipsed about the house
trailing the silken scarf,
playing dress up ~
the scarf now a little worn,
now a little faded,
its translucent white now a bit gray
with age, like her hair,
and the brightly colored pastels
like flowers and butterflies
now a little softer,
yet her treasured old scarf
still made her smile,
and a tear fell when she saw
her grownup daughter's eyes light up
as she lifted the silky folds from the tissue
with joy of remembering
those childhood moments so clear,
this scarf so cherished;
it was worth every penny.

It lies now across a child's pillow,
the drifting ends
spreading and flowing gently,
wrapping around her small head
as she sleeps,
her breath a little ragged,
like the abstract pastel colors
that still looked like flowers and butterflies
dancing upon the translucent white silk
like her skin, tinged
with the grayness
of illness, of treatments;
she alone wages this war within,
she alone withstands stares and whispers,
when her crown of strawberry hair
is lost in this battle.

The day the last lock falls,
her mother gives her
a small tissue-wrapped gift,
a hand-me-down,
a remembrance of child's play,
of traipsing about the house
trailing the silken scarf,
playing dress up,
now worn
now faded
now softer
and her eyes light up
as she lifts the silky folds,
of her Grandmother's pastel scarf,
and the flowers and butterflies
dance so proudly,
and she smiles.

It was worth every penny.

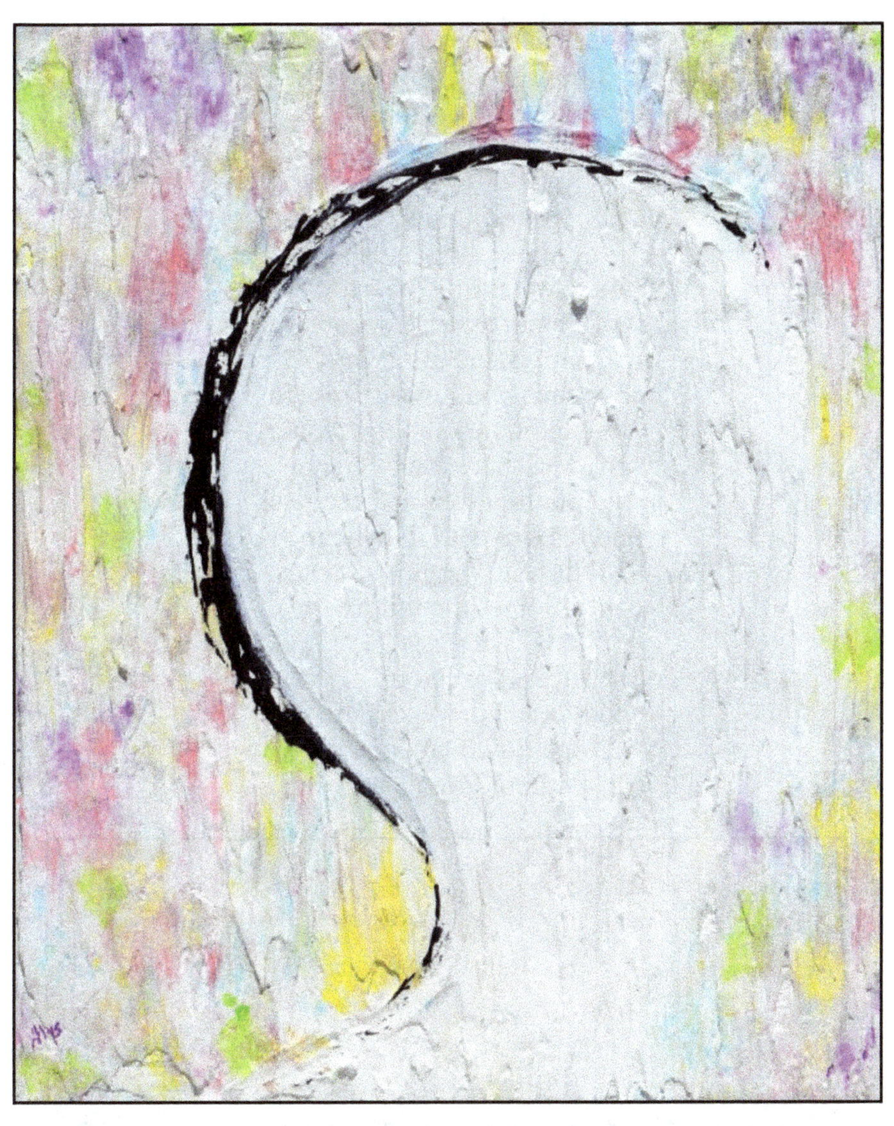

What If

What if I loaded up my car
and took a drive somewhere
away down an open road
to live where I've never been ~
a little house in a woods
with a long silent lane,

or a shack at a southern shore,
a houseboat would work,
or a quiet motel
(at least for a day or two)

what if I packed up
some of my stuff ~
some clothes and the little desk,
the coffee pot and my special mugs,
my pillows and all of my boots,
my paints and favorite records,
my medicines and my dishes,
my tools and rocking chair,
old photographs and recipes,
and the big pot I use the most,
I'd have to dig up the roses,
(but I'd miss the willow trees)

what if I loaded up my car
and took a drive somewhere
away down an open road
to live where I've never been . . .

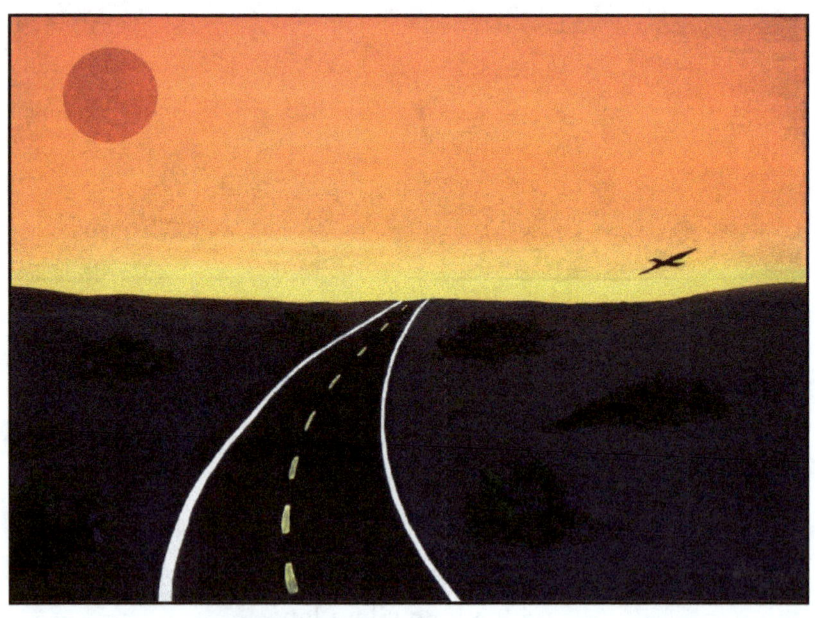

Summer Storm

Overhead the sunset sky
echoes that white hot
shimmering reflecting line
on the ribbon of road
stretching forward
to a darkened horizon
then a flash
a hundred miles away
signaling the storm
waits for me.

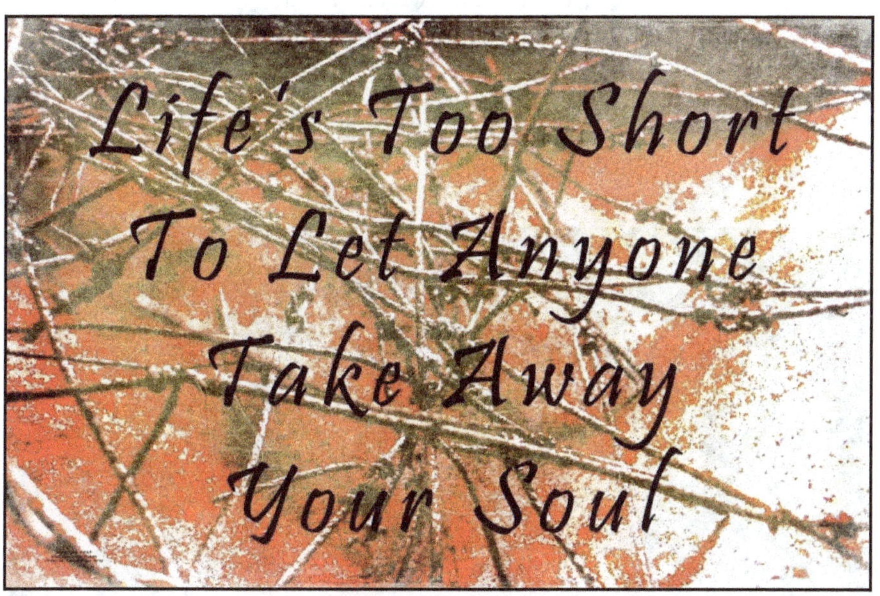

Dubbed In

There was a time
when I couldn't see
any face but yours,
and there was a time
when the only voice
inside my head was yours,
and there was a time

when all my words
were bonded just to you ~

but somewhere
along this lonesome path
different words let loose
in the voices of my ancestors
within an abyss of colors
dark and light,
and other faces came into view;

and when my eyes
are tightly shut,
I hear their voices shout
echoing with joy ~

"*Forget you!*"

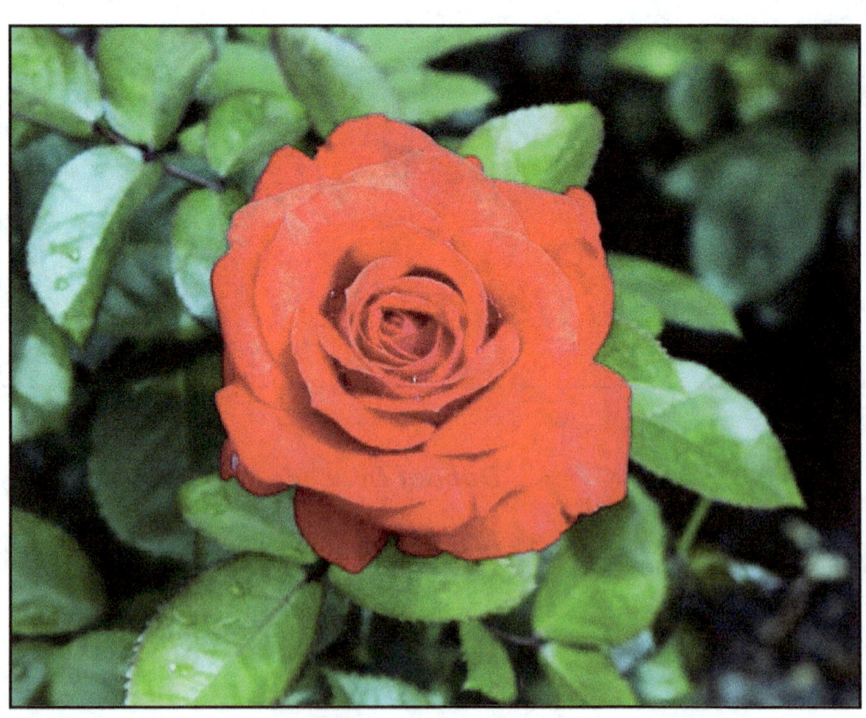

She Blooms

She blooms,
like no other,
from within the greenest leaves
and thorns protecting,

I breath her in,
a sweetness overwhelming,
cloying and dancing,
a torrid delight,

straining like pulp through damp
and sickening air;

yet, she blooms, like no other ~
my red summer rose.

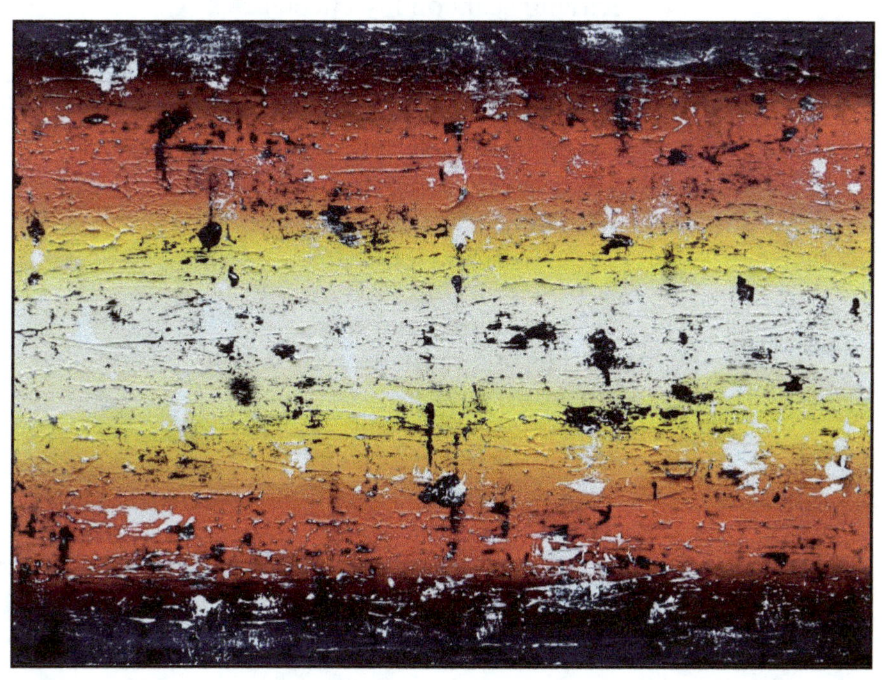

Bugs In Amber

Moments flee
like a gas station robber
cutting down that hourly wage
without warning
into nothingness
taking that life with no explanation
(who cares anyway what the alleged need?)
moments flee
trying to escape
the trap of time.

Last Summer

Rain fell mercilessly that day;
in a torrent, a summer rain,
rare and hard like a hatchet strikes,
like sharp tears
leaving scars on my cheeks
as I planted your favorites
around the totem you carved;
now the cutting rains save me,
bringing lushness and wonder
to this year's falling rain.

Time indeed moved on,
scarring over this rusty wound
still aching and raw,
the scar itches and burns slowly and sure,
blanketing tomorrow in dread,
like fog at dawn creeps across my landscape;
today is consumed,
today becomes reliving sorrowful days
of yesteryear.

Time indeed moved on,
without you.

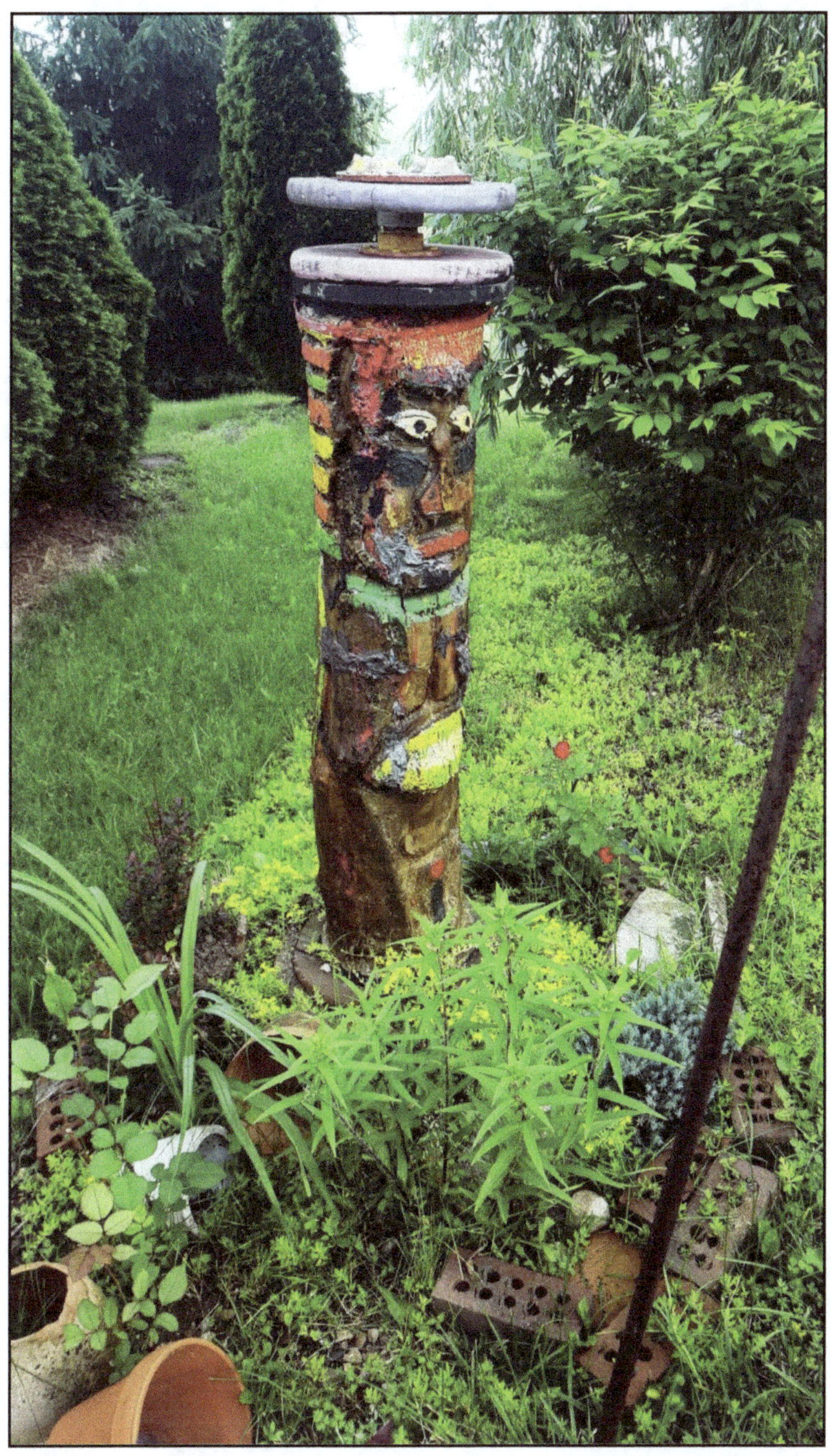

Rollercoaster Ride

trying to maintain
an even keel out there

wishing to hide
the darker side
the sadder side
deep inside

up up up
then
down down down
rolling around and around
curves too sharp too fast too much

intoxicating
nauseating
breathless

trying to maintain
an even keel out there
laughter freezes
sticks like glue in my throat
a heartbeat change to tears
because

I still see that split second
I still feel that sinking sickness
in the pit of my stomach
as the rollercoaster
roared on through me
that fractioned second
when life left your eyes

trying to maintain
an even keel out there

my rollercoaster ride
a year later

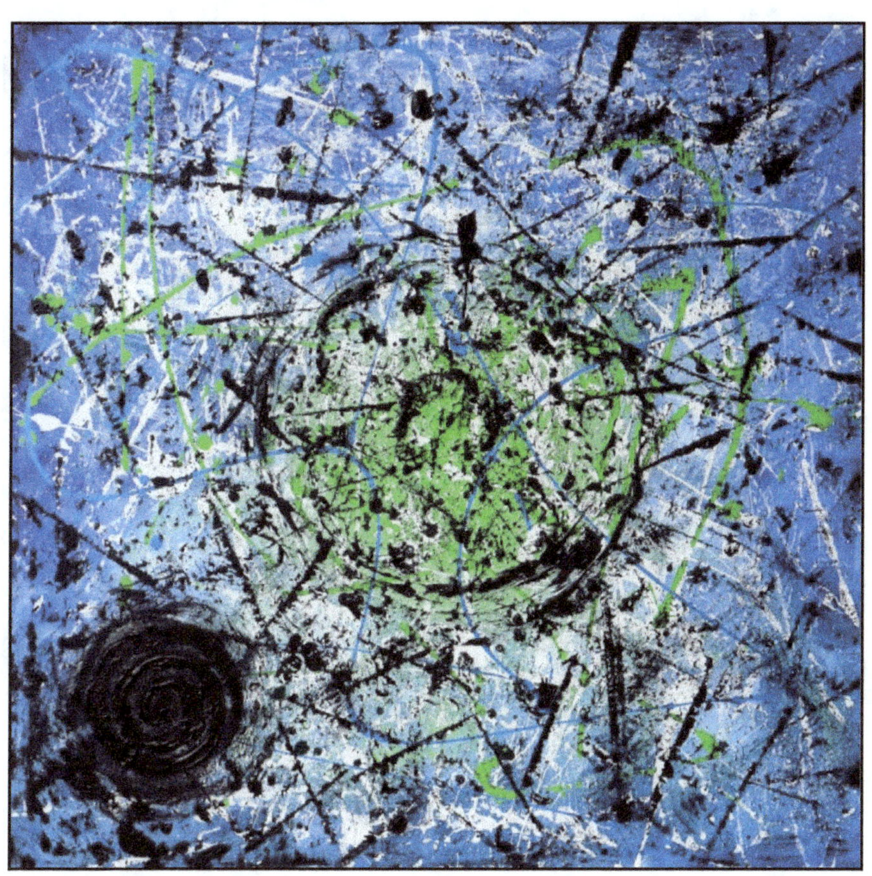

The Green And The Blue

Am I in the green and the blue of you,
the cosmos of chaos of you,
the expanding universe of you,
the lightning flash of you?

Are you in the blue and the green of me,
the chaos of cosmos of me,
the universe expanding of me,
the flash lightning of me?

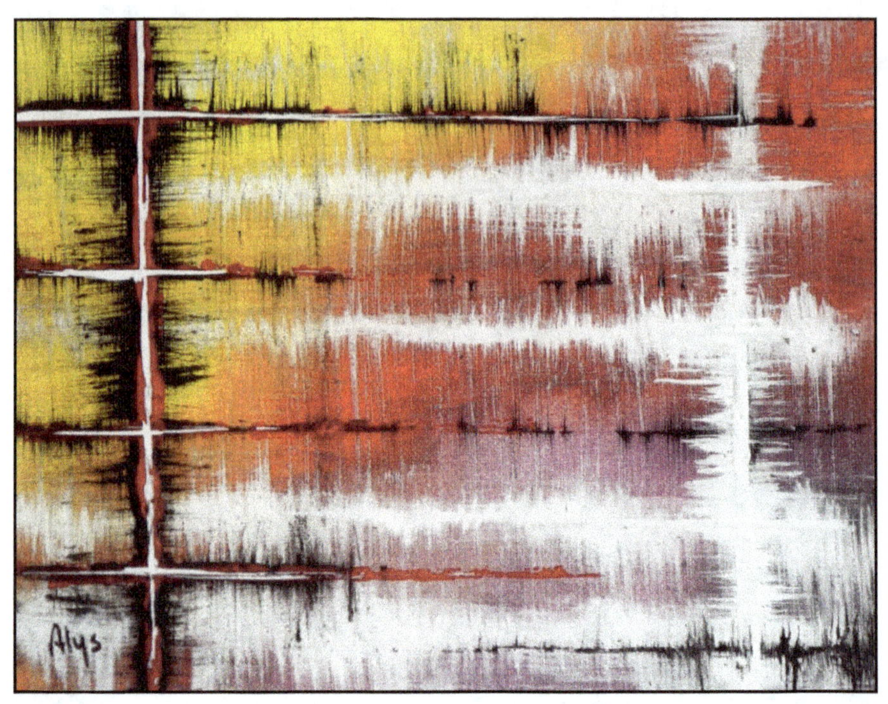

Microwave Heart

It always starts
with simmering,
anticipating
mingling flavors,
heat slowly rising,
enticing ingredients
to dance together,
blending within
bubbling sauce,
floating aromas
permeating,
wafted
intoxication.

In minutes now
a microwave
beep beep beeps
its tinny notification.

Halfhearted half-dead flavors,
mediocrity in a bowl,
just instant depthless apathy
and tepid scent.

The bowl's always
way too hot
to touch.

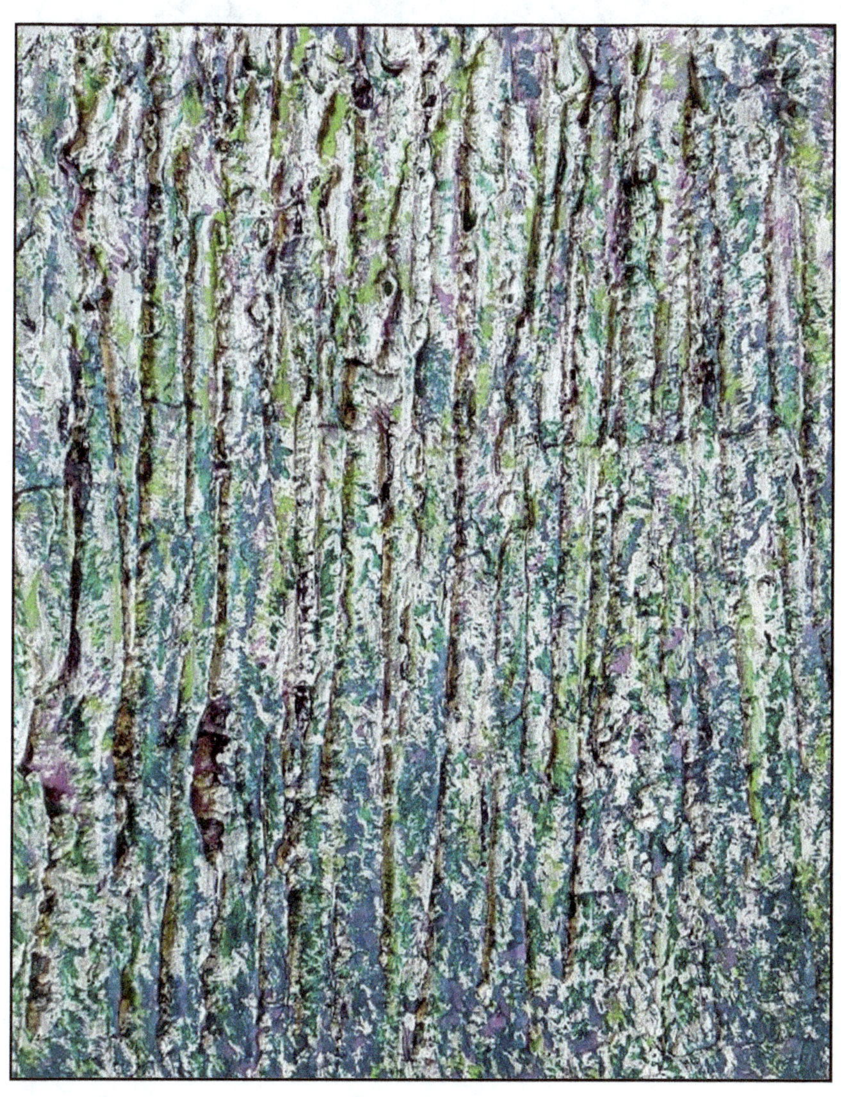

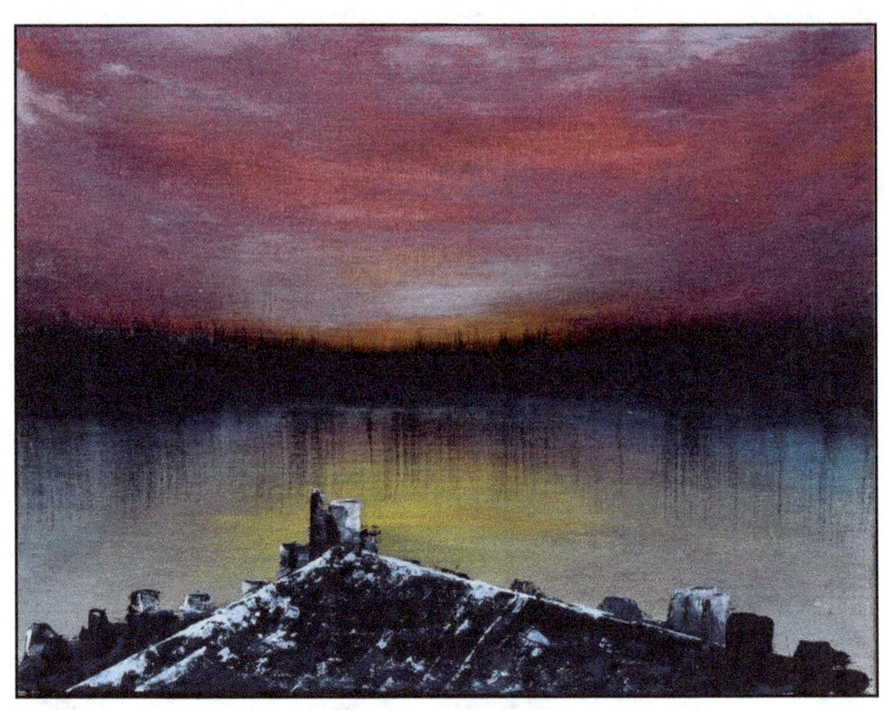

Another Day

If I had a dock to sit upon
by a golden bay
I'd sit and wait forever more
and never would I stray

If I could watch the rolling tide
crashing out and then back in
I'd watch and wait forever more
and never leave again

If I could waste another hour
with you right by my side
I'd waste and wait forever more
in eternity to bide.

My Irish Toast

May you always find comfort,
May you always find peace,
May the dawn lift your heart
from sadness so deep,

May a light shine bright
in your darkest night,
May the sun warm your bones
no matter how far you roam.

Here's to a tranquil night,
and whiskey tomorrow.

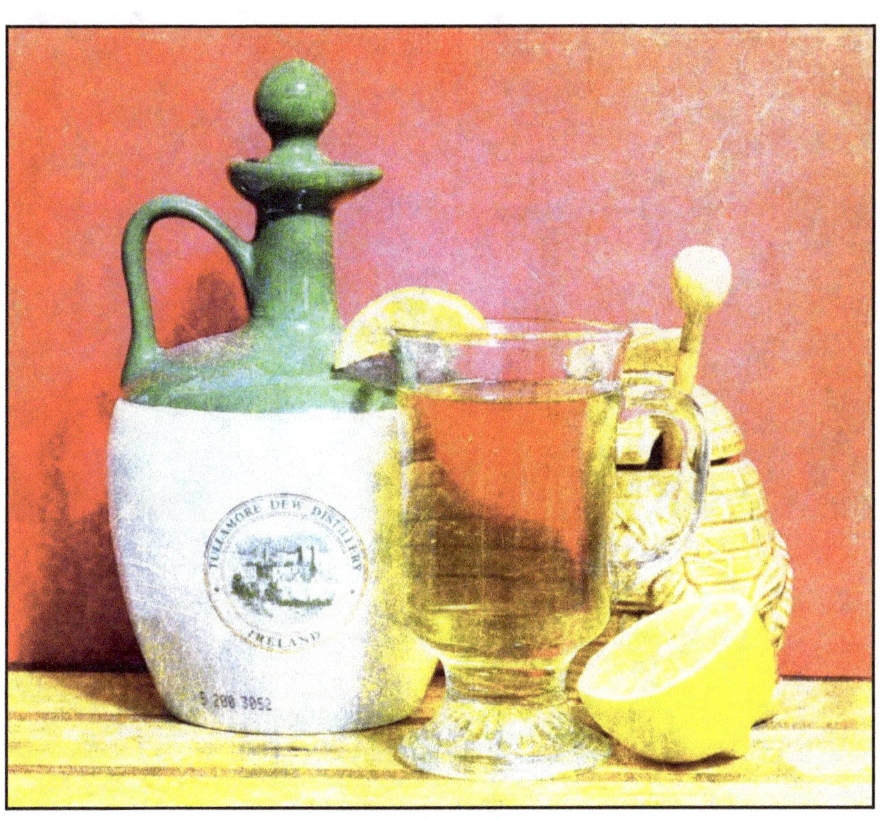

Waiting

She waits
as dawn breaks blue
like a little boat
rocking
gently

~ remembering ~

~ dreaming ~

~ waiting ~

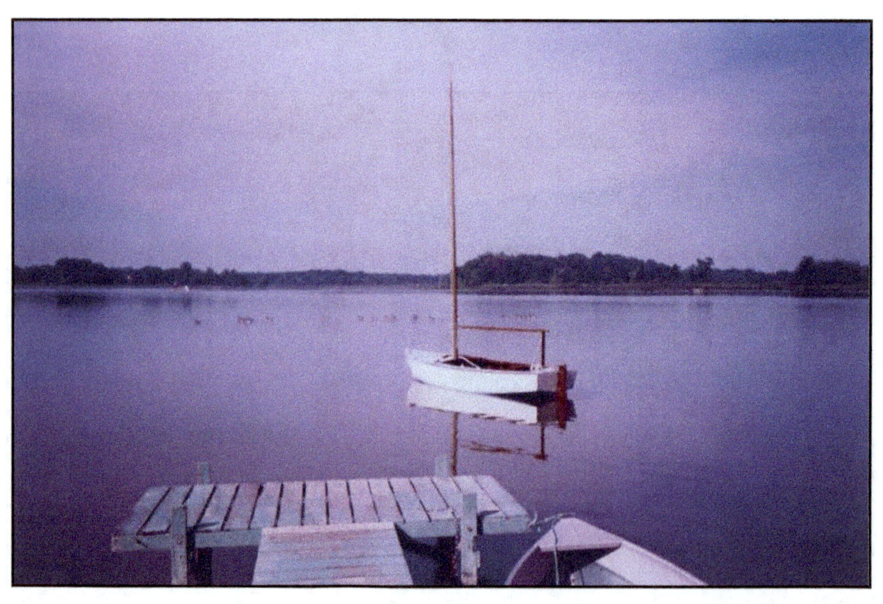

Buttermilk

In a lifetime of skies,
all those whites and blues
of a million days,

in a lifetime of skies,
in the reds and pinks and yellows

of a million dawns,
In a lifetime of skies,
mingling with a million purple sunsets
turning black,

in a lifetime of skies,
you rarely get
buttermilk clouds.

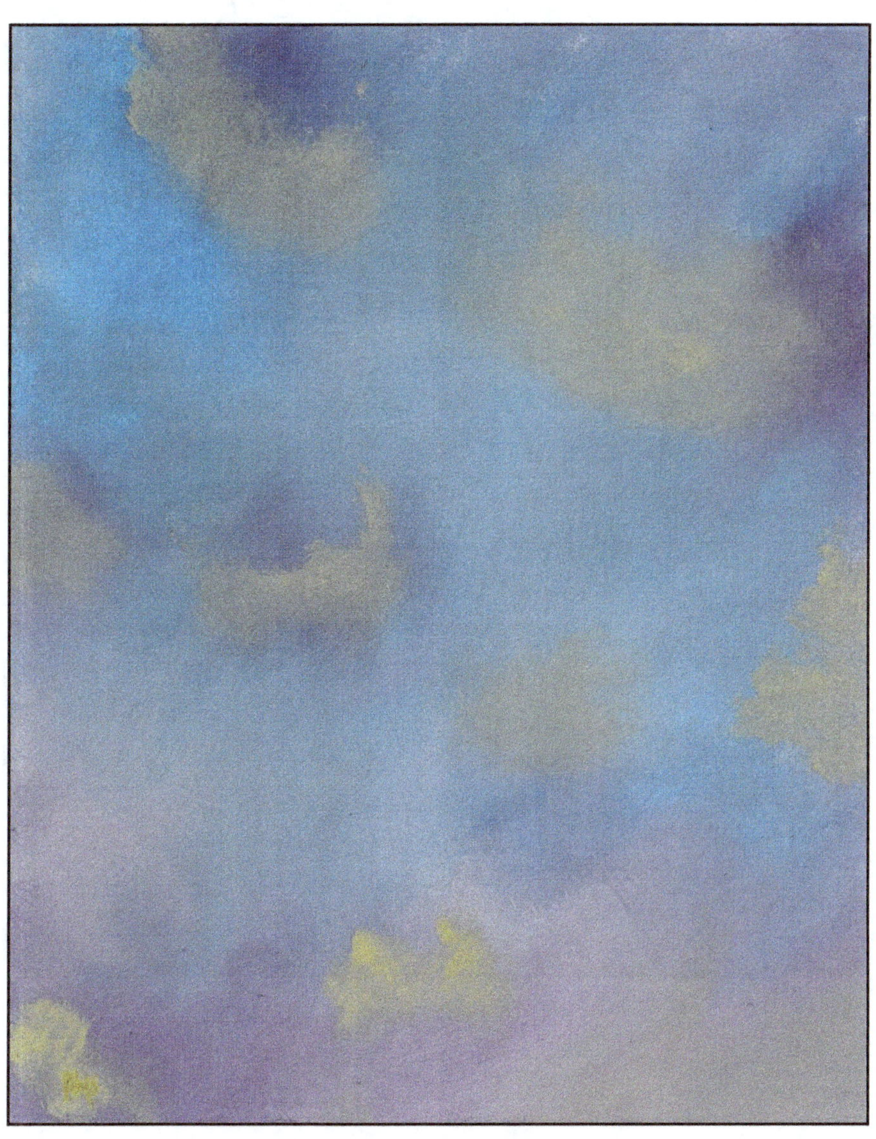

Counting

thunderclap crashing
one mississippi then two
a room sits empty

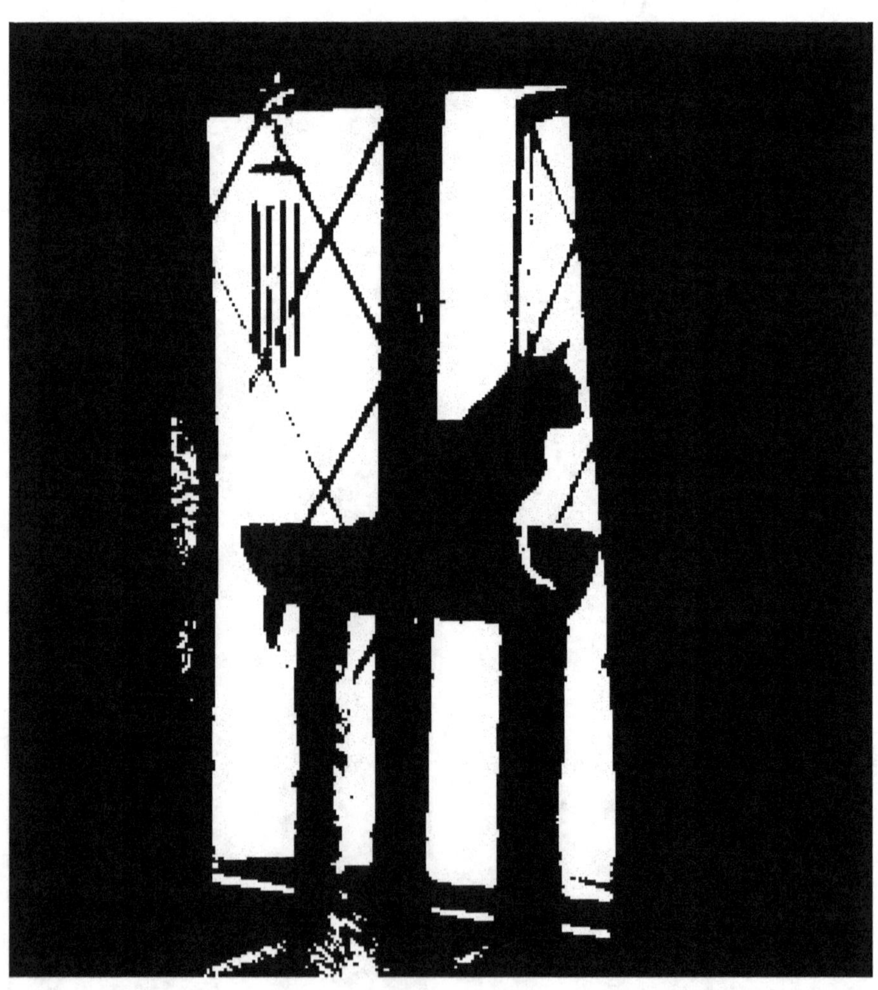

The Rowan Tree

She grew
almost inadvertently,
a little too near
the cliff's edge,
near that
one
broken rock,

she grew
alone,
overlooking the sea,
like a woman
waiting,

alone,
wrapped in worry,
waiting
for a ship to return.

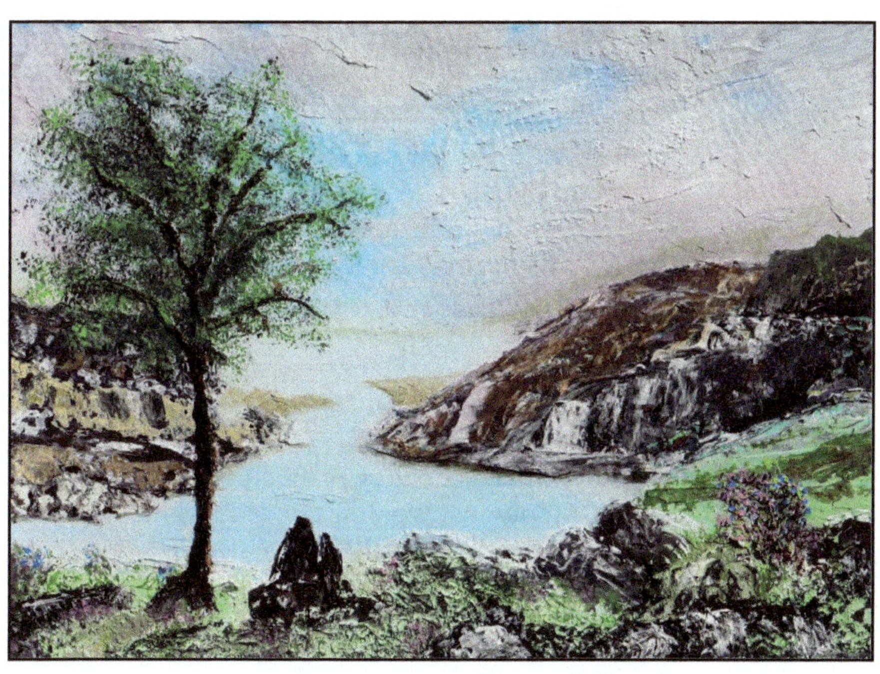

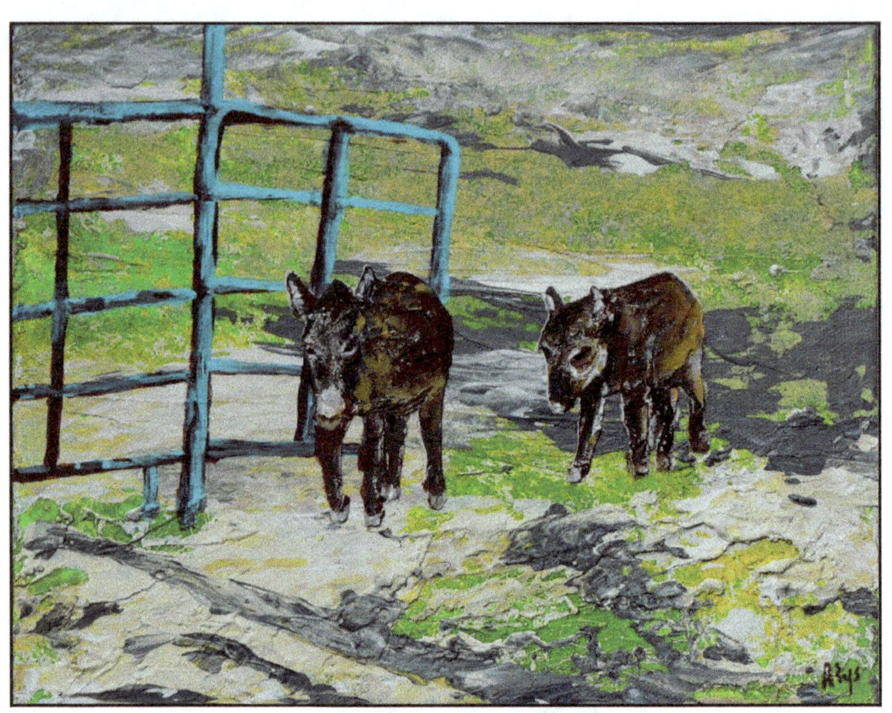

At The Farm I

There once was a donkey so tiny
with hooves that were ever so shiny
no matter who'd shout
he'd amble about
with a look that said, "just kiss my heiny"

At The Farm II

There once was a donkey named Fred
who simply just wouldn't be led
'til the dinner bell rang
with a really loud clang
then he ambled right back to the shed.

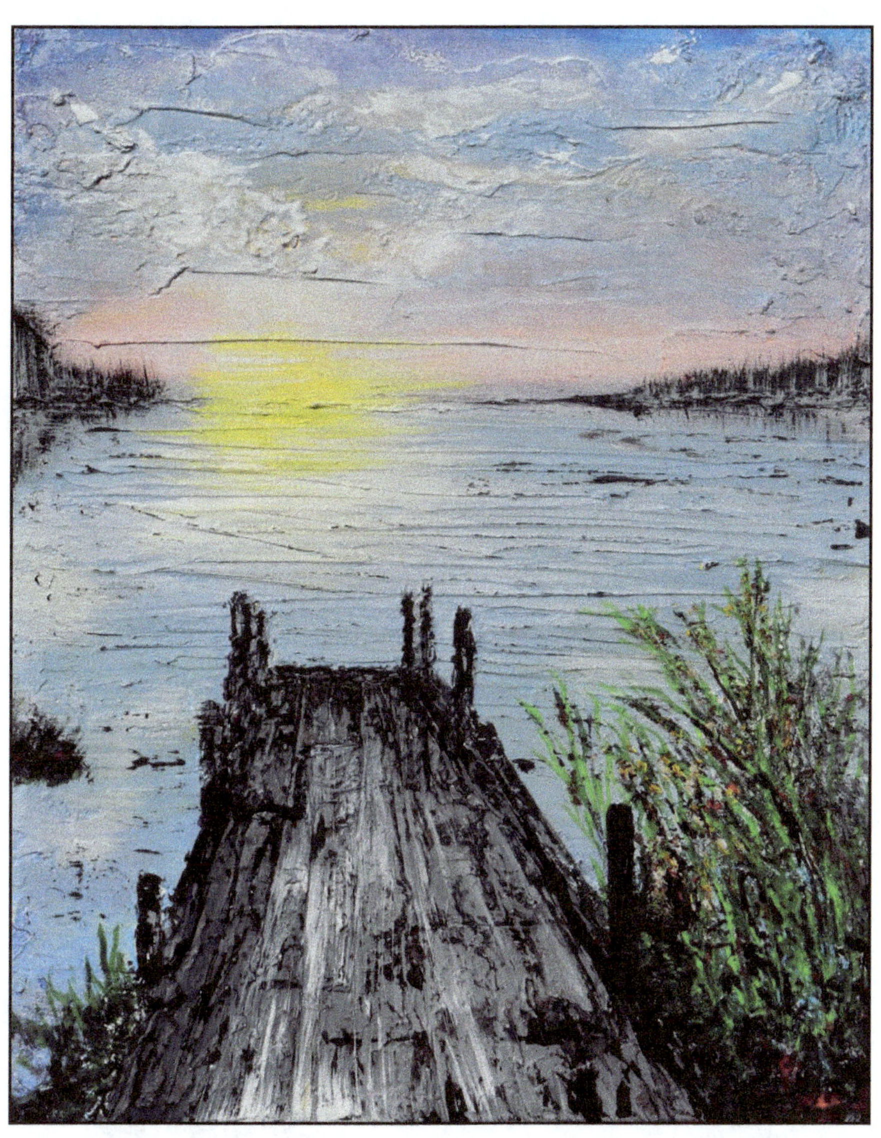

At The End Of The Day

As you lay down your head at the end of the day,
as you close shut your eyes with a drifting sigh,
as peace descends like a soft dark blanket,
let your last thought be
I am loved.

Anyway

The candles shook and flickered
Within the deadened air,
Obediently they came to her
in silence loud and clear;

Whispered sounds surrounded me,
Voices from the past,
Shadowed forms fell through me
as her spell was cast;

She turned the cards, revealing
A man swinging to and fro,
Then a Tower crashing down,
And I felt your piercing soul;

I saw beyond her ribbons,
And her mottled lace,
I saw my past and future
In your Devil's face;

Yes, I saw the hand she dealt me,
When Destiny had her say,
Forever warned, forever warned ~
I turned those cards anyway.

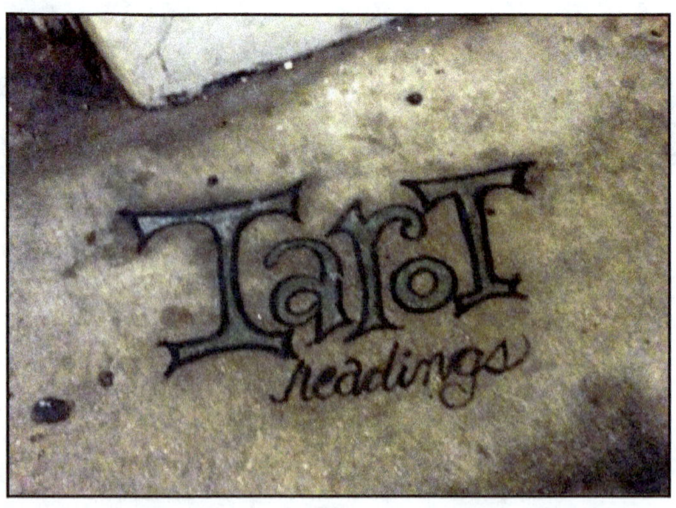

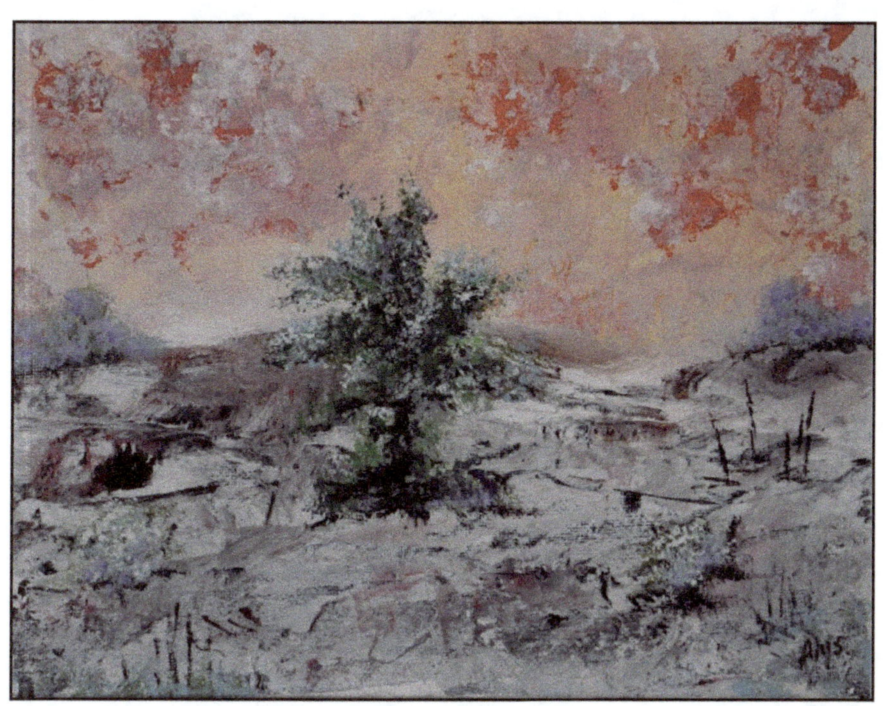

In The ICU Waiting Room

attention focused for any change,
even slight, even imagined;

holding a prayer's breath,
gaze shifting for a moment;

watching the gray and somber parade,
joyless, marching to and fro;

muted chimes ring out
just beneath the normal noises in here;

a happy pink or blue moment
when a baby's born.

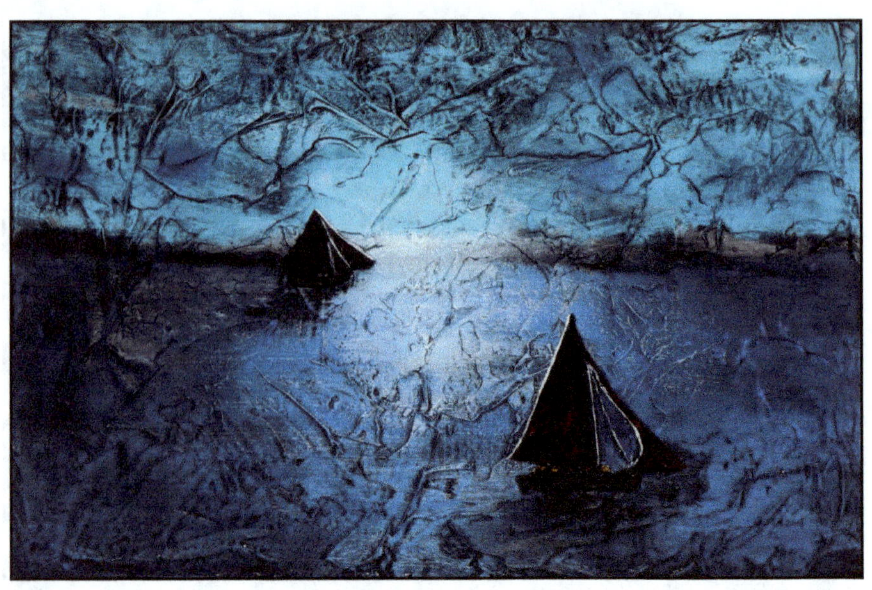

Moonlight With Galway Hookers

Came sunset on the water,
silent as ancient graves,
rolling with the hidden moon
comes softly rocking waves;

gliding sliding side by side,
our red sails slowly fill,
the secret moon calls us on,
as clouds hang thick and still;

the Galway shore fades away,
a moonlit course appears,
my landlocked soul sighs content:
set free, my fever clears;

with slicing bow, every roll
between water and wind,
moonlight guides our destiny,
sailing, sailing onward.

October Leaves

I heard my name called out
within the bluest sunlight,
crisp air swirling about:
lifting dead leaves' dancing flight;

once more I heard my name
an echoing from the past,
steady and just the same:
your voice held me still and fast;

through jeweled leaves I gazed
through orange and gold and green,
to bluest sky unfazed:
I see your eyes still twinkling.

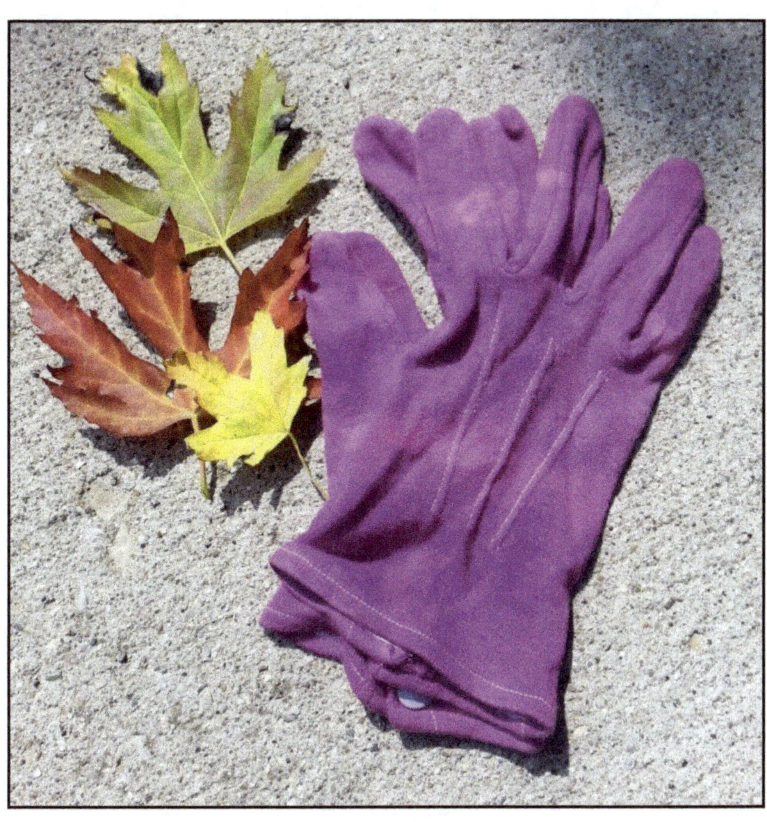

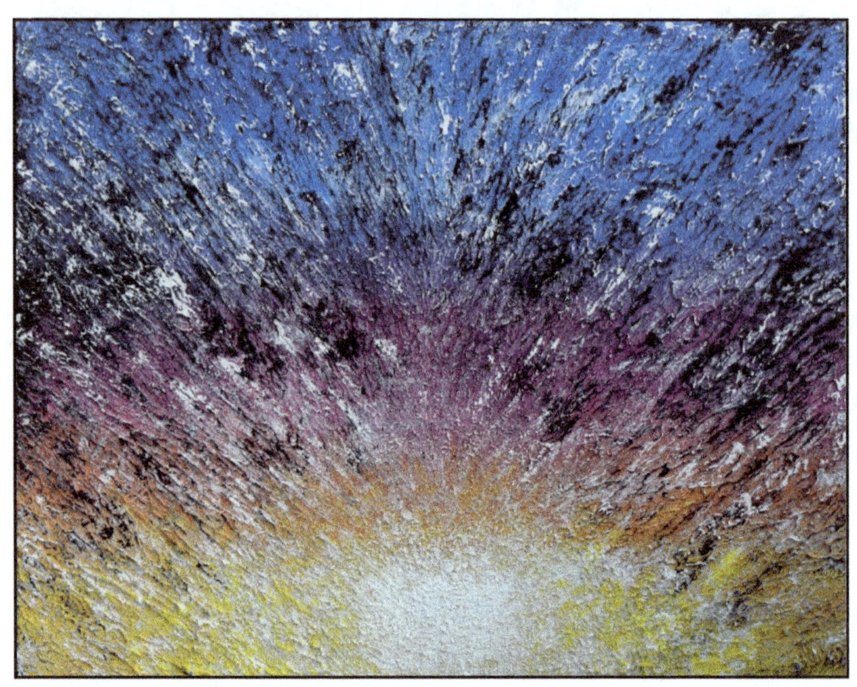

Pride And Joy

breath knocked out
always in a rainbow
a plurality of generations
dancing in the sunlight
becoming light
becoming warmth
love
eternally
pride and joy

Temper

that elusive degree
that melting
~ play it out ~
slowly yielding to the heat
as you stir

~ do not stop ~
moving towards the flashing moment
a fragile explosion
of temper

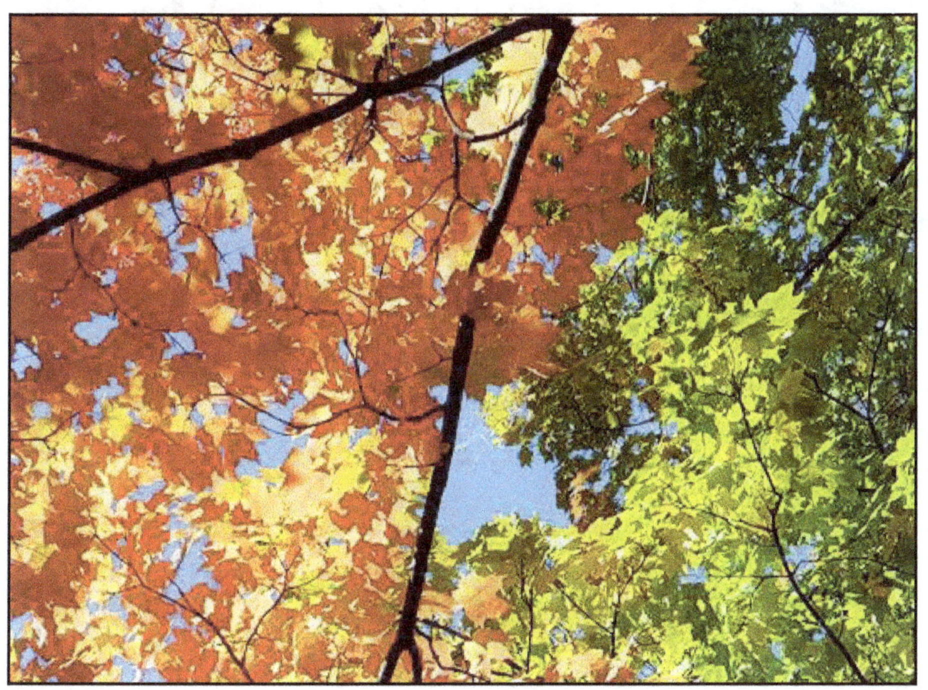

The Last Dance

morning's cold air bites
Fall crumbles into Winter
a lone sparrow sings

as a crisp Wind stirs
wearing colors of the Sun
a pretense of warmth

yellow, red, and gold
falling leaves dance to their deaths
in bitter silence

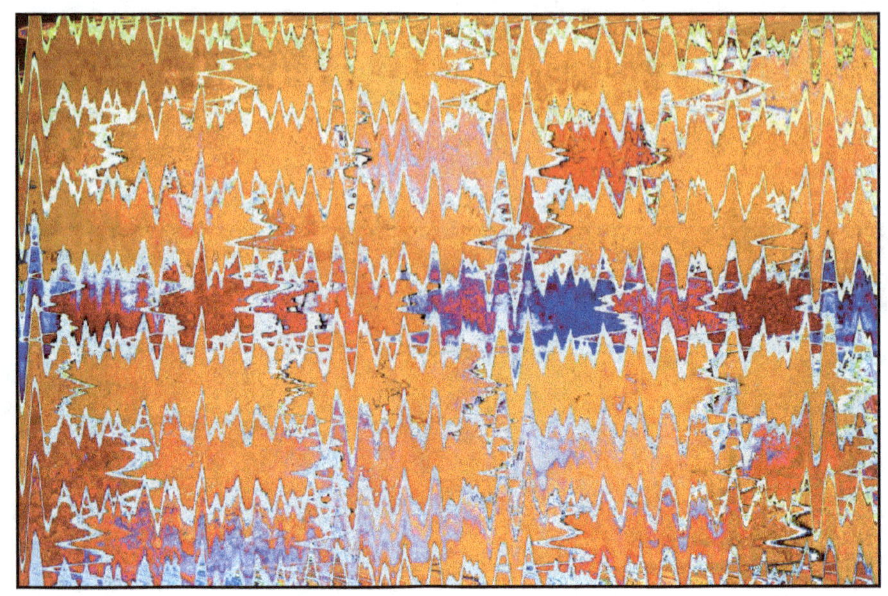

Fever

O Fever Fever, go away,
I have too much to do today,

some other soul I wish you'd find
to torture and drive out of mind,
I've had enough, I'm just sayin'
of your constant fever'd games a-playin,

it ain't nice and it ain't fun
so with yo' bad self away please run,

I wish to walk alone today,
I wish you'd listen to what I say,

you're not my friend, you're not my lover,
you're stalking me and always hover
'round my body, heart, and head ~
honestly, I wish you were dead!

Short Skirts

a faint warmth in the air
blows in Spring and brings
short skirts snapping
tightly-wrapping
curving asses asking for grasping
or at least turning heads
as long smooth legs taper down
to sandal-clad feet with painted toes
laughing with youth
and confidence and firm skin

I used to wear short skirts
oh yes I did
laughing with youth
and confidence and firm skin
and when I walked
they snapped
kissing the faint curve of my ass
a teasing hint where my long smooth legs
began their descent a slow burn tapering down
to my sandal-clad feet with painted toes
a faint warmth in the air
blows in Spring and brings
short skirts snapping
reminding me
of the heat of youth

but now
my skirts are longer and no longer snap
caressing the faint curve of my ass
gently draping down
softly covering and hovering
around my legs
my legs are eternal
smooth and long enough
to wrap around you

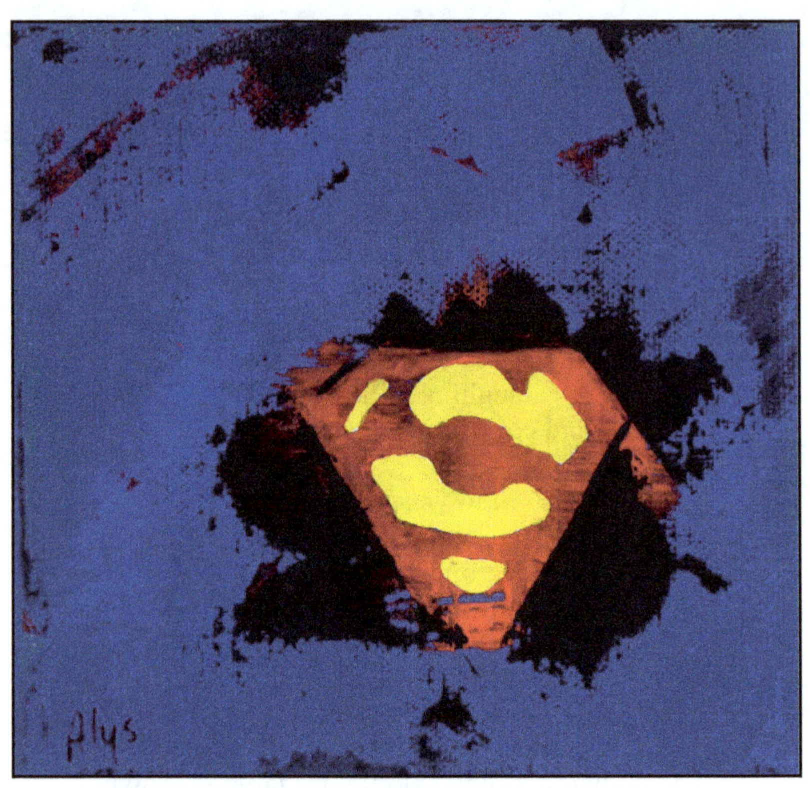

He Told Me

We texted a lot that week,
back and forth our sorrow filled messages flew,
mine reaching him at work,
his finding me in a hospital room,
where my father's life was slipping away.
Holding it together
for my mother, my brothers, and my children,
at some point my resolve dissolved
and I cowered in a hallway texting him
my hopelessness and despair,
and he wrote back:
you're the strongest person I know.

I went back in, shoulders squared;
with six words, he carried me.

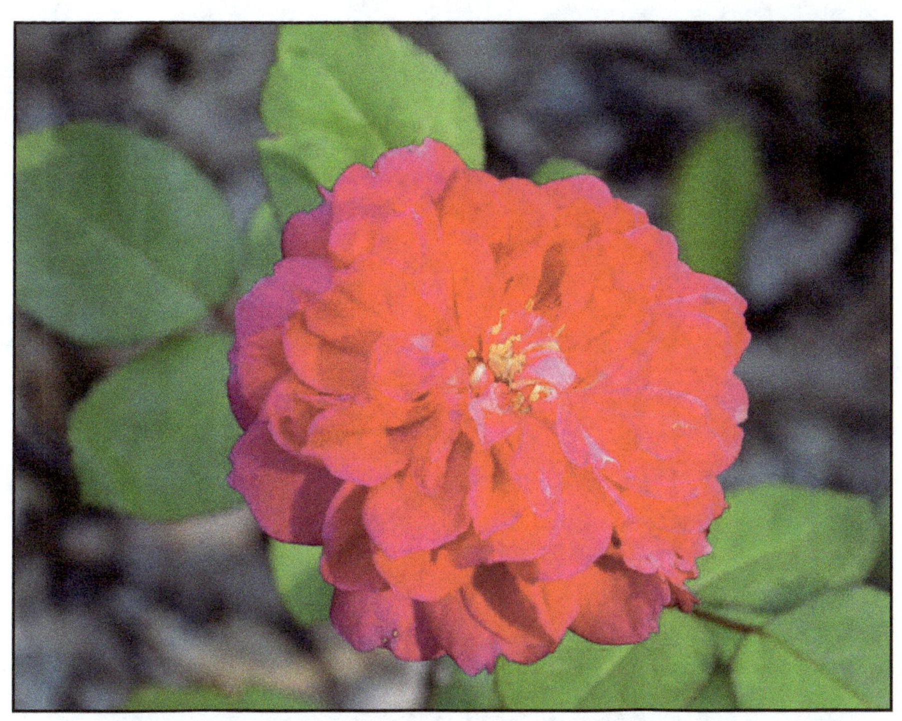

Awakening

petals unfolding
seeking sunlight soft or hard
her soul expanding

sunlight burning white
soft breezes with yearning blow
her soul escaping

night falls gently down
diamond stars dancing above
her soul expanding

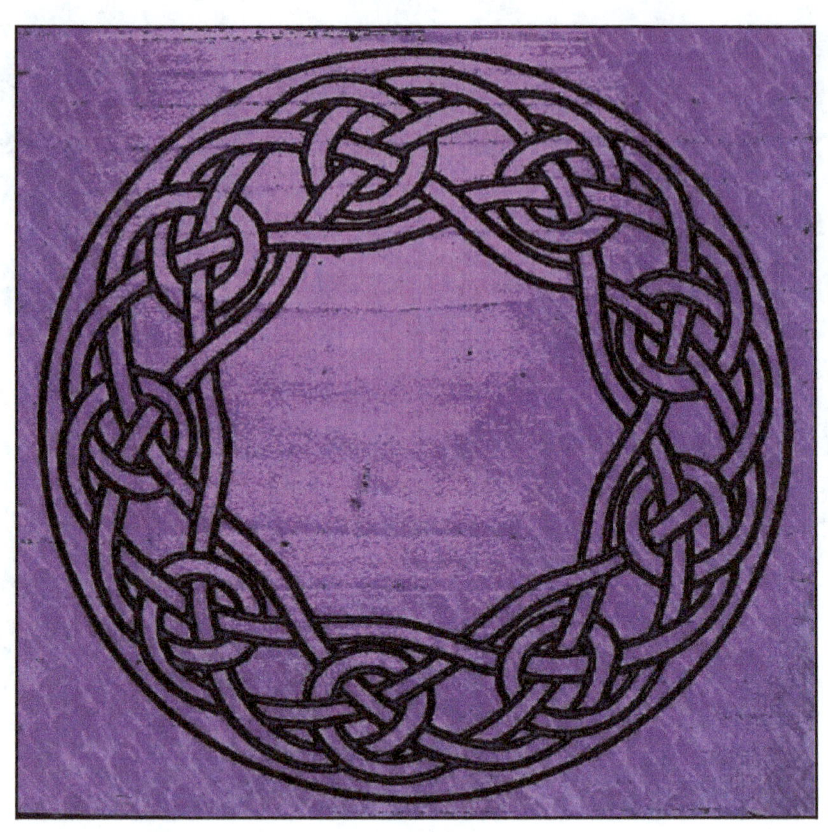

Caim

May You be a bright flame before me
to see my way in Darkness,
May You be a guiding star above me
so my Path might yet be clear,
May You be a smooth path below me
for my weary Feet to tread,
May You be a loving Guide behind me
with whispered words Encouraged;

May You journey right Beside me,
Today, Tonight, and Forever.

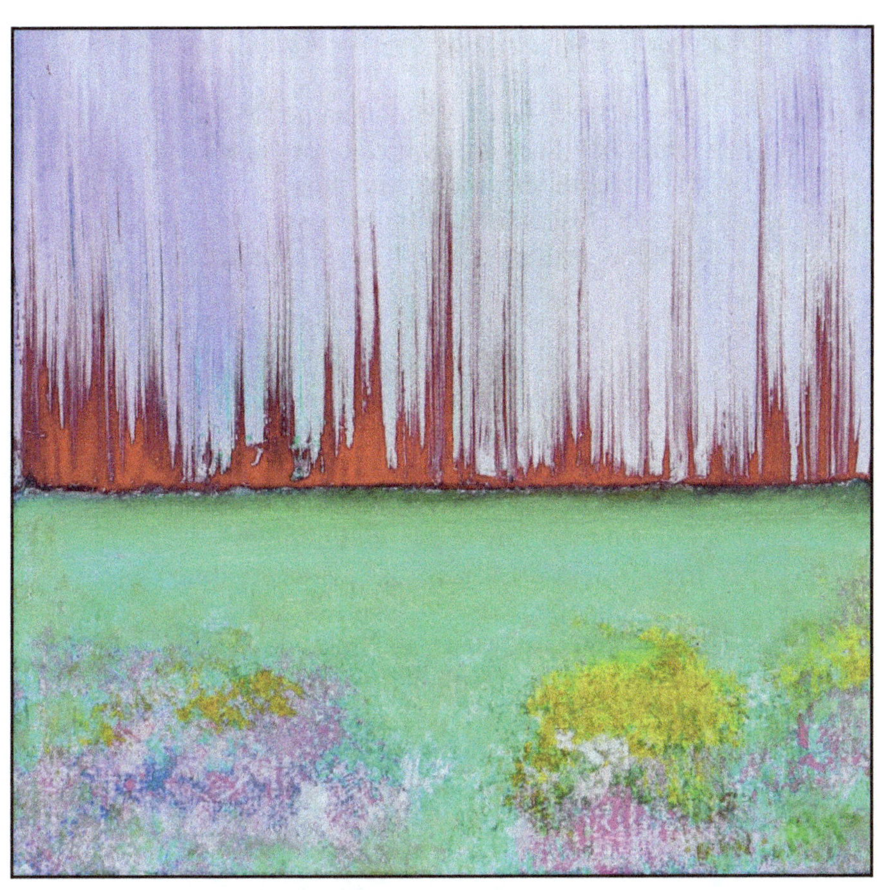

Sunrise I

clouds slowly moving
late Winter dawns in red streaks
coffee mugs warm us

Sunrise II

clouds slowly moving
early Spring dawns in red streaks
coffee mug warms me

A Poem for My Friends (or) An Epic Limerick

There once was a woman named Alys
who lived in neither hovel nor palace
she read more than most
researched pillar to post
making others regard her with malice

Try as she might to stay silent
for she wished not to affront
neither stranger nor friend
nor fabric to rend
but at some point she just had to vent

Into the fray she would tumble
irregardless of storms that would rumble
she'd speak her mind
and ask questions in kind
quite loudly with ne'er a mumble

There were times when she pissed people off
and derisively snorted between every cough
for she had no patience for lies
or the annoyance of flies
and away she swatted them both

Like Alice, she thought it nonsensical
and stressful upon her right ventricle
when they'd sputter and spout
like the Red Queen would shout
For God Sake Off With Her Headricle!

Now 'tis true that Alys was smart
and true that she had a good heart
but they said the thoughts that she thunk
and considered opinions all stunk
as if she had let out a great fart

So Alys considered retirement
to escape the risk of bemirement
in their coagulated muck
(she gave not a f*ck)

and off for a dark beer she went

The reactions of others notwithstanding
the ridiculousness seemed overwhelming
she'd fought the good fight
so called it a night
(kinda just like Peyton Manning).

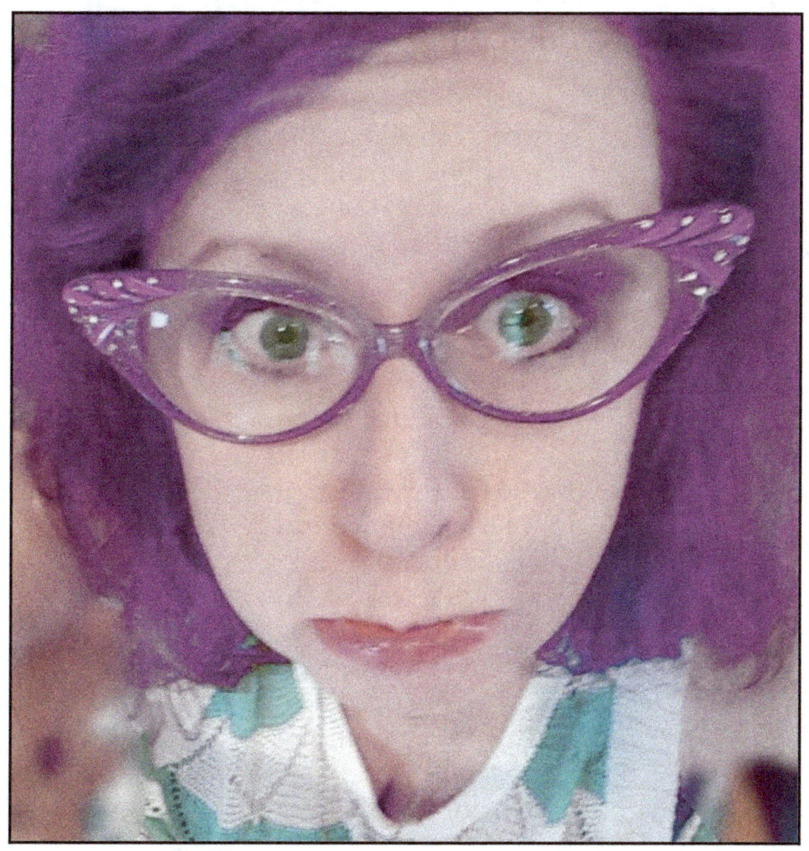

My Aged Ways

Shy hesitation
did not well serve me
in my youth

when I gave in
and gave up
all too often;
my soul enslaved.

Battle-scarred aggression
did not well serve me
in my middle age

when I fought angrily
against anything
and everything;
my soul at war.

From time to time
I still hesitate in shyness

and from time to time
my battle scars
hurtle me forward angrily,
like a Pachinko ball
pounded
pillar to post,

but mostly now
I am quiet
in my soul.

Such are my aged ways.

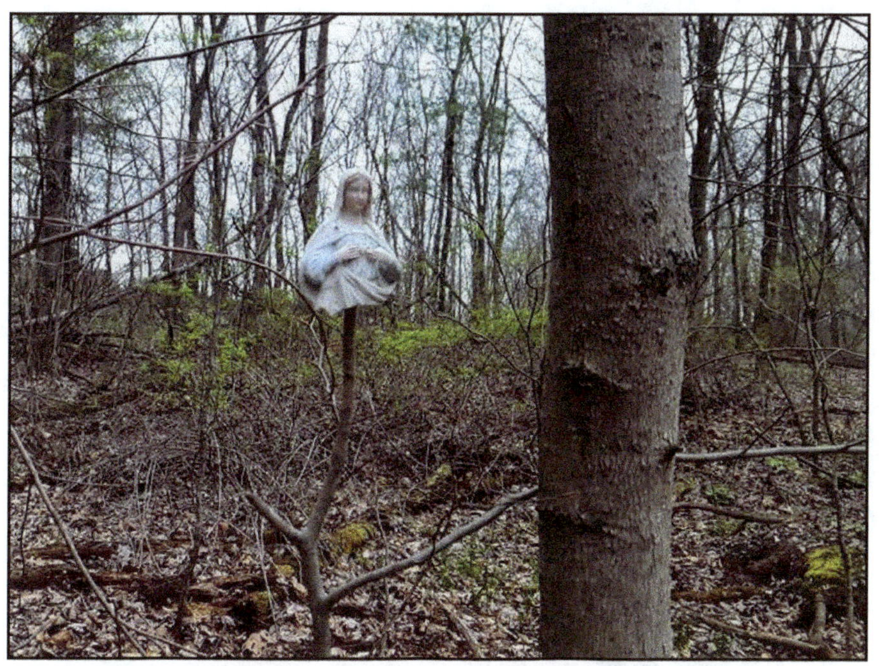

(photo credit Tom Vernon)

Broken Mary

Whether by grief torn asunder
(her loss her most grievous loss),

or Mother Nature's wrath
(for the old gods die hard),

or the sins of humankind
(our ever-destructive footprint),

she remains fully resolute
in her halved condition;

ever vigilant.

Untitled I

steep heatwave rises
wafting roses fragrantly
fifty-three years on

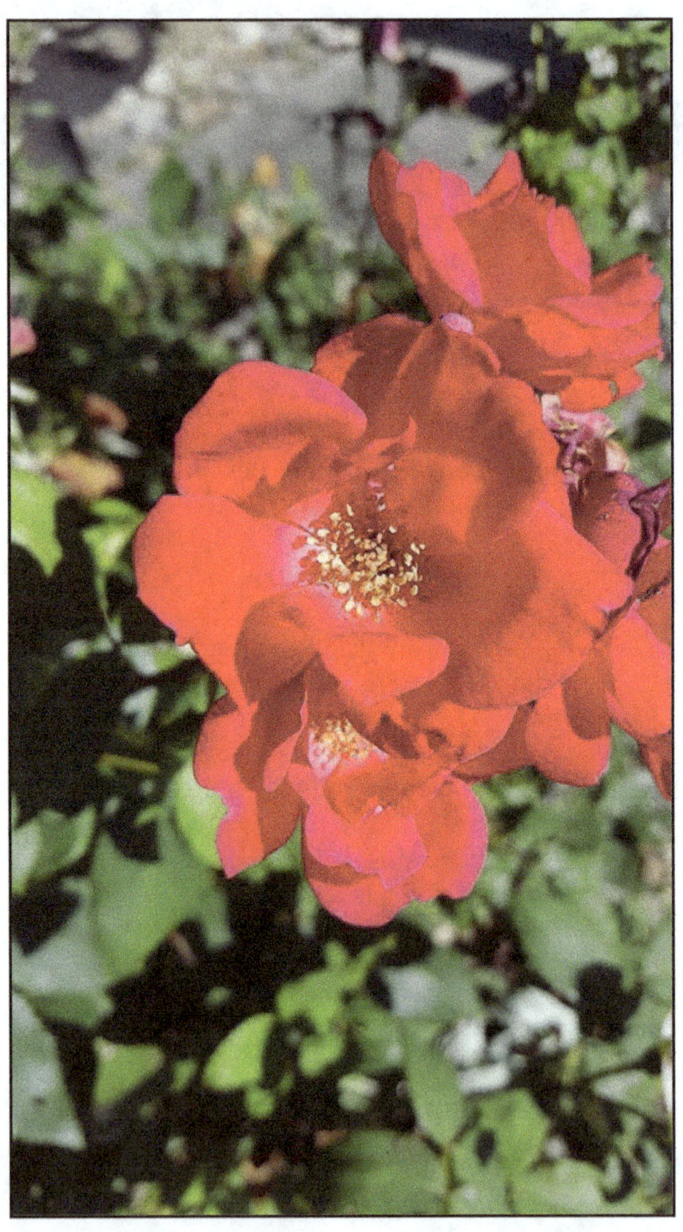

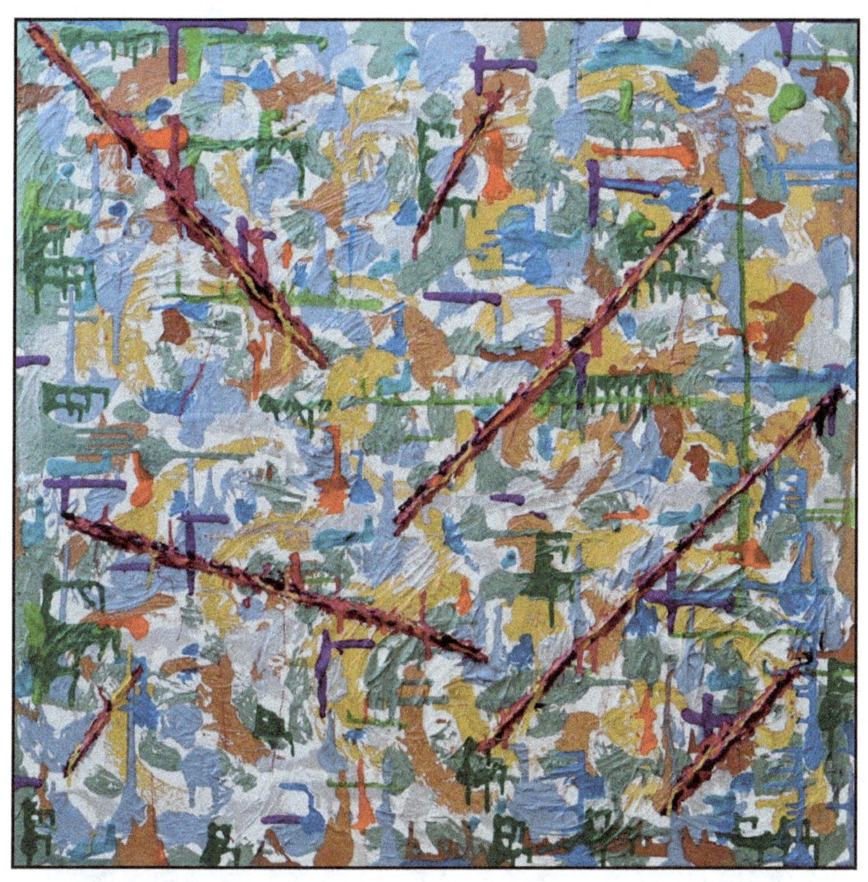

Stepping Closer

Each day I step closer
to an edge unforeseen by most,
it is thin and gray and tough,
and sheer and invincible and fast.

Somedays I step
with caution and careful tread
tinged with dread,
goosebumps crawl over me,
as I am mesmerized by the abyss.

Somedays I step
almost running ready to throw myself

across and through and into that thin gray veil,
because I know what waits for me ~
a safe haven at last.

Stepping closer,
I peer over it into vastness
unknown and known
unremarkable and remarkable,
an embracing unfriendly infinity.

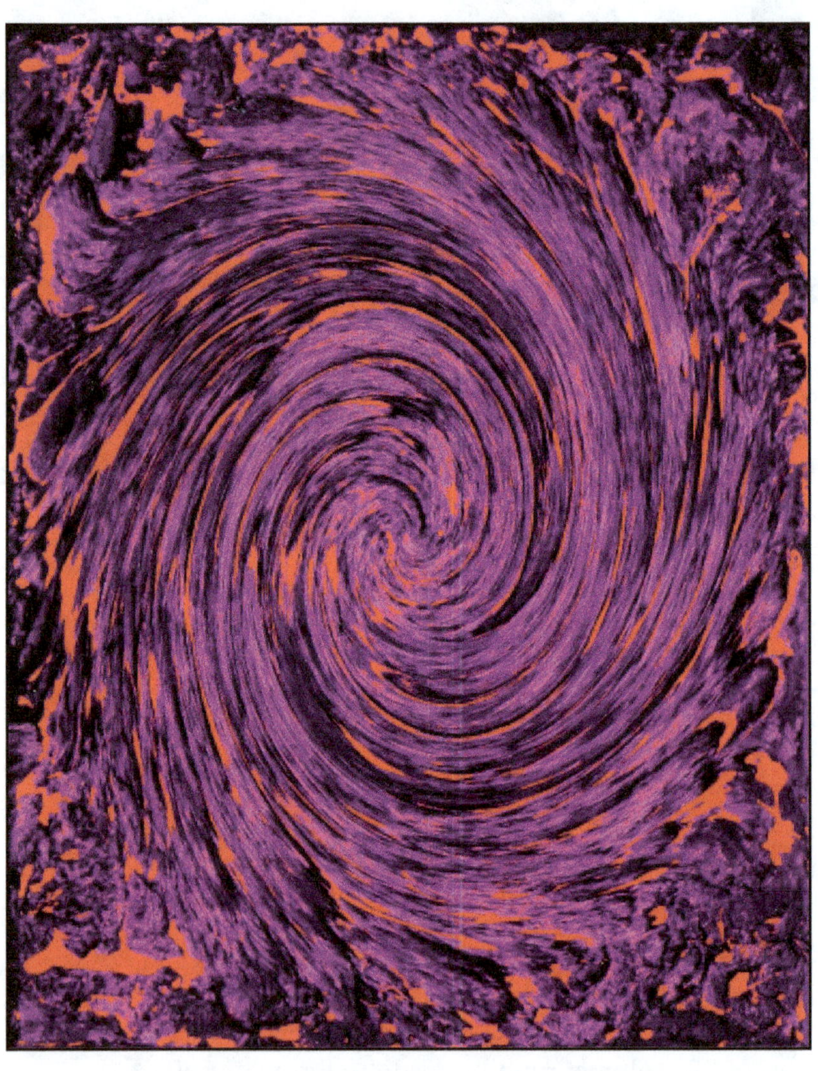

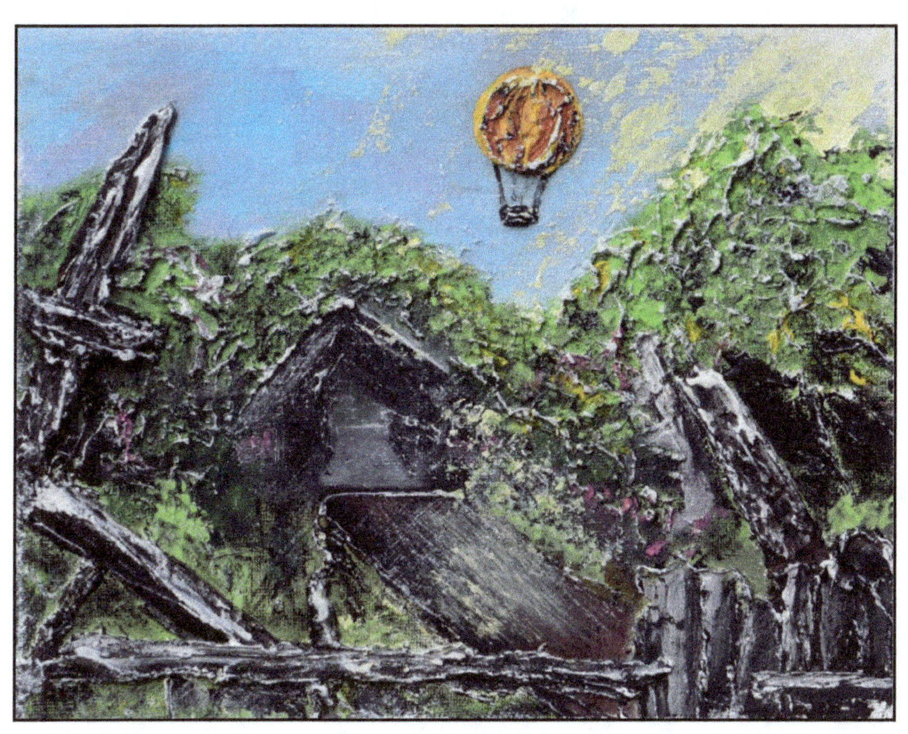

Liberty Fanfare

Sunset on the prairie
symphonic prayers
lofting away
like the hot air balloon
released
sailing
skyward
to France.

Jurassic Park

Somnolence rolling on and on then
BEHOLD!
~ running from dinosaurs ~
eyes closed we sway . . .

E.T. The Extra-Terrestrial

each note becoming
an element
a single part in the building
of an extraordinary
alien device
rendered into crescendo
thus his dream fulfilled

"E.T. PHONE HOME!"

Star Wars

stirring sounds fill the air
and we transport at lightspeed
with a flash of stars
fragmenting
falling
into a galaxy far far away

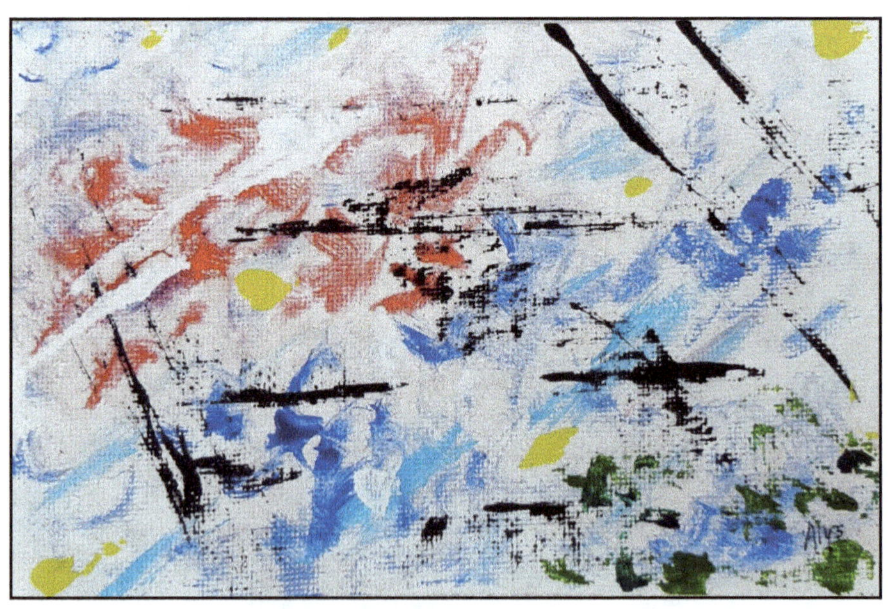

Harry Potter and the Sorcerer's Stone (Hedwig's Theme)

delicately flitting flitting
destination a destiny;
she flies true
bringing The Magick
with a feathered flourish.

Raiders of the Lost Ark

with the first notes
I weep,
remembering;
with the last notes
I smile,
remembering.

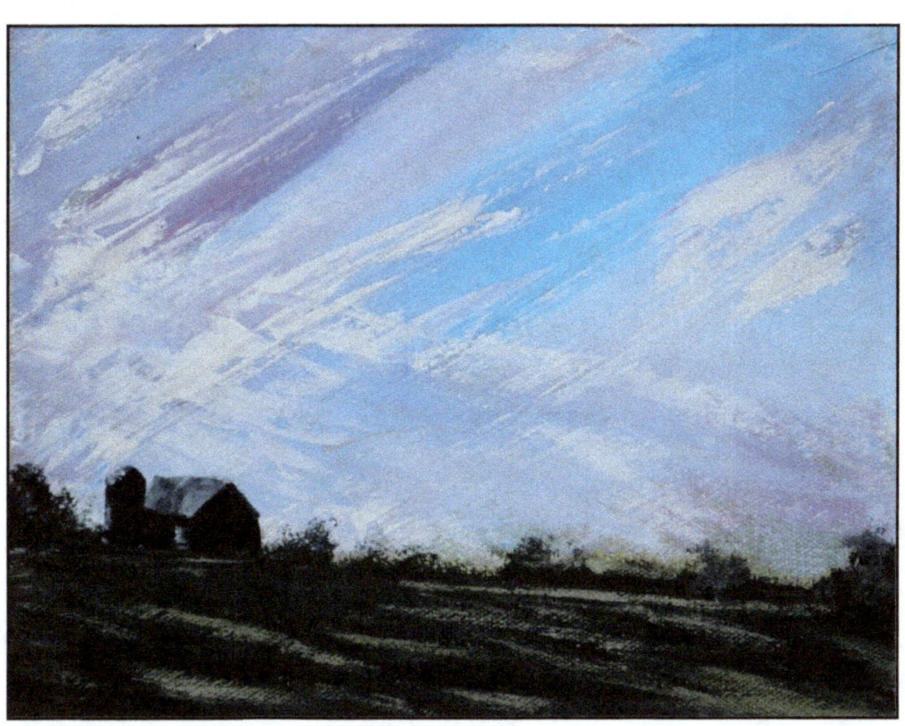

Grief
(in memory of my dad)

Time indeed moved on,
scarring over this rusty wound
still aching and raw,
the scar itches and burns
slowly and sure,
blanketing tomorrow
in dread,
like fog at dawn creeps across
my landscape;
today is consumed,
today becomes reliving
sorrowful days
of yesteryear.

Time indeed moved on,
without you.

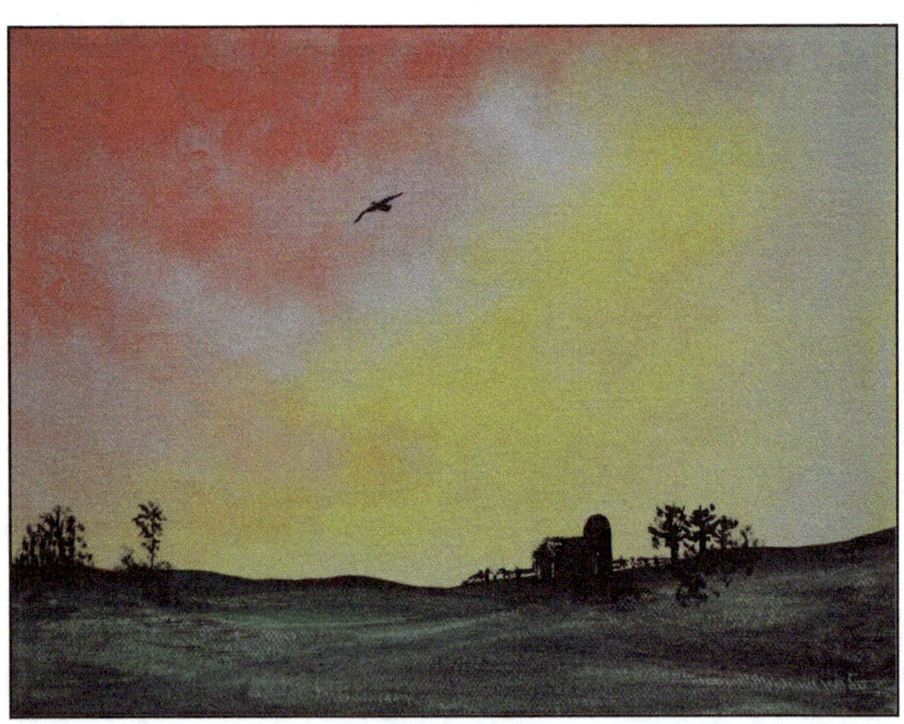

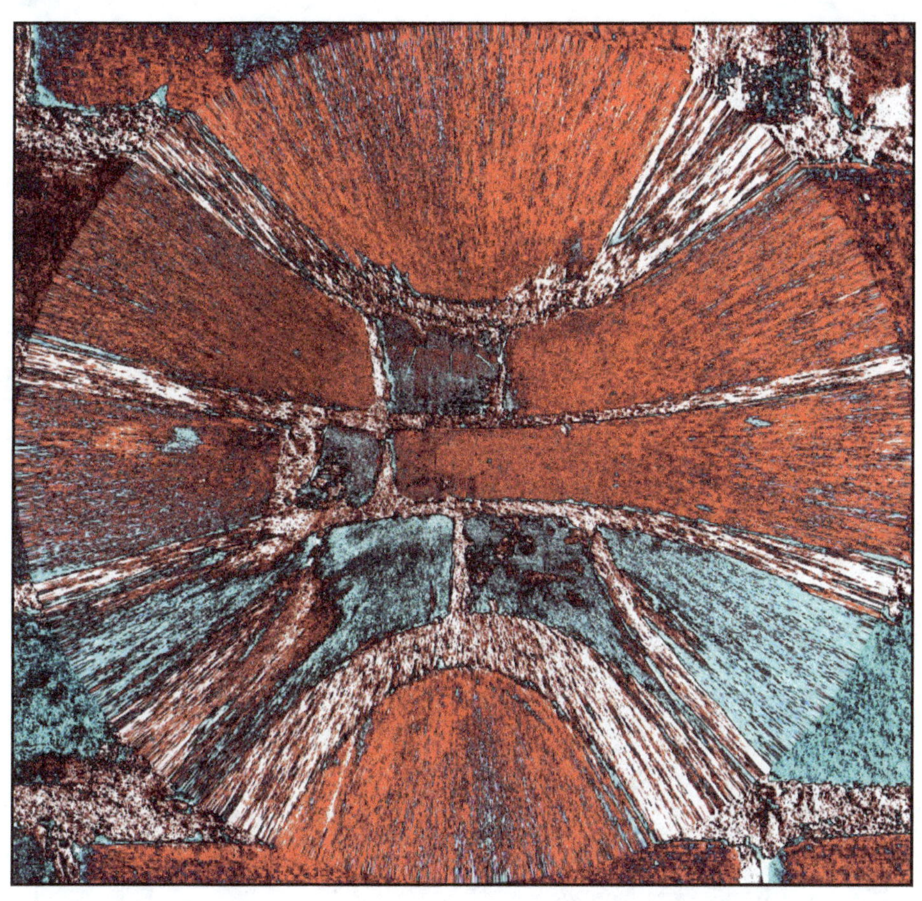

Oi!

Fever fever go away ~
I must run around today;

Up above the world so high,
My fever reaches to the sky,
And makes me feel all itty-bitties,
Confusing all my favorite ditties;

Fever fever go away
I don't like this game you play.

Untitled II

sunrise over the trees
meets songbirds' rusty warbles
a birthday cake waits

Untitled III

(something is) too high
for where I am tonight
(someone is) too dangerous
for where I am tonight
(somewhere is) too far away
for where I am tonight

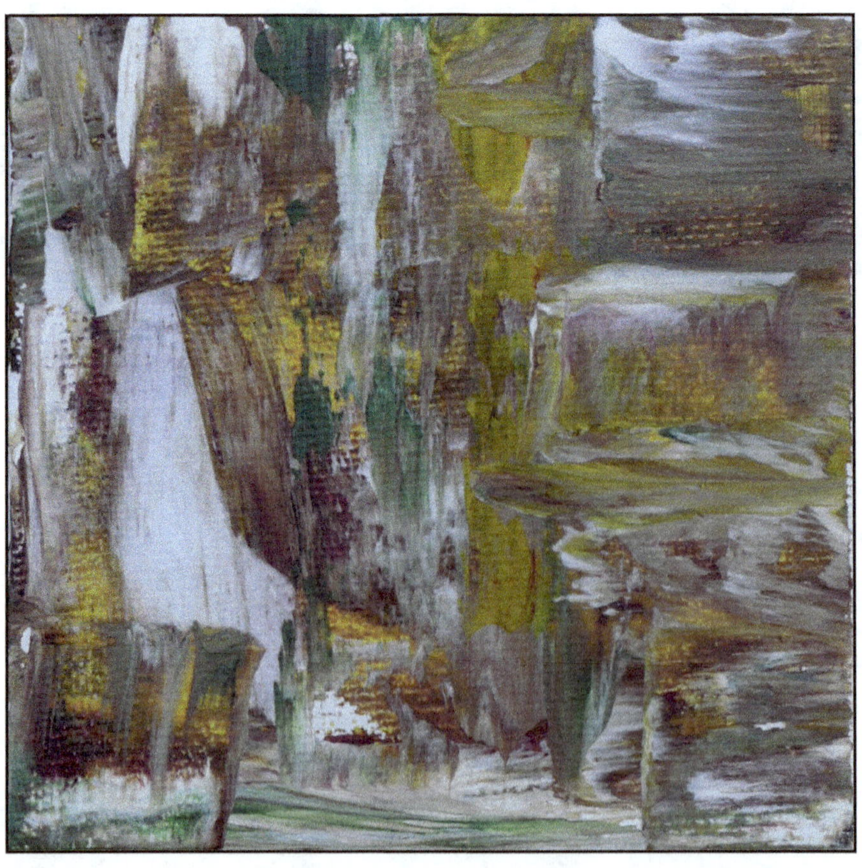

Sometimes

I can't see the forest
through the trees;
edges blur
and confound my senses;
I wander
aimlessly
shamelessly.
Who the Hell are you?

Cracks

Tectonic shifting
deep within
lifting this surface;

cracks
like laugh lines
appear
here and there
signifying
age and wisdom;

and now
here and there
rising
toe-stubbing
nuisances
become unavoidable

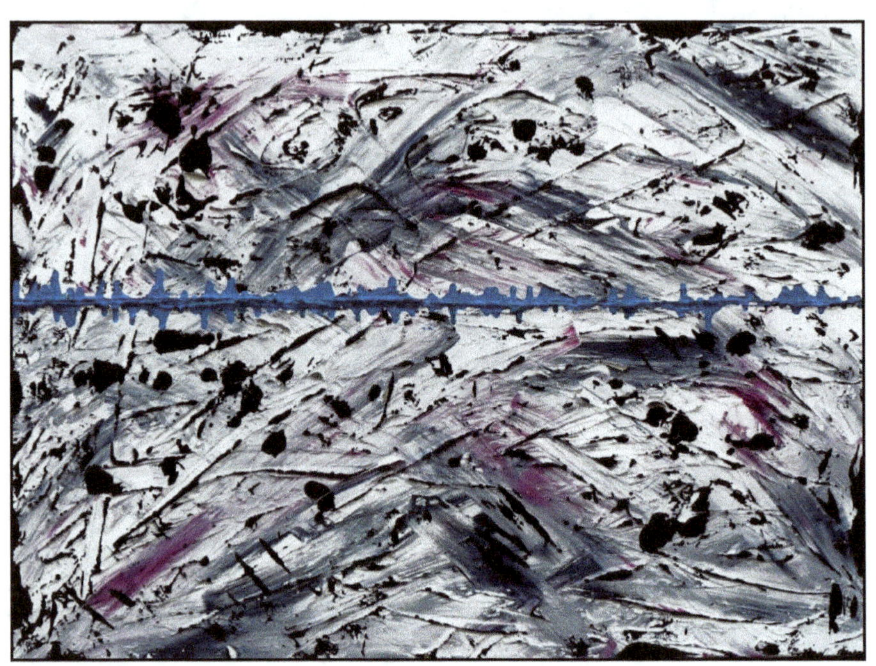

Lines

Does demarcation rule us?

Splitting us
along lines,
defining us
with labels;

dividing and conquering,
boxing us in,
keeping us out
of each other's way,

keeping us out
of each other's hearts.

Remembering I

(a Birthday haiku for Jim)

far-off thunder rolls
softly falls the Georgia rain
brown-eyed boy is born

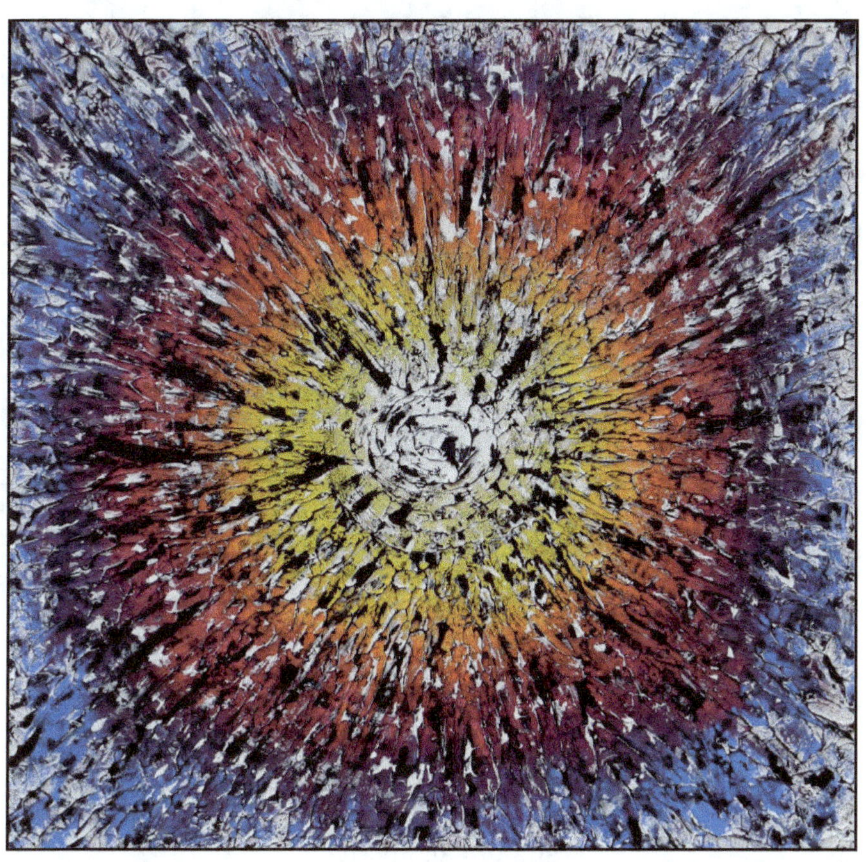

Remembering II

(a Birthday haiku for Phil)

pine trees and red clay
humid air presses to earth
steadfast blue eyes flash

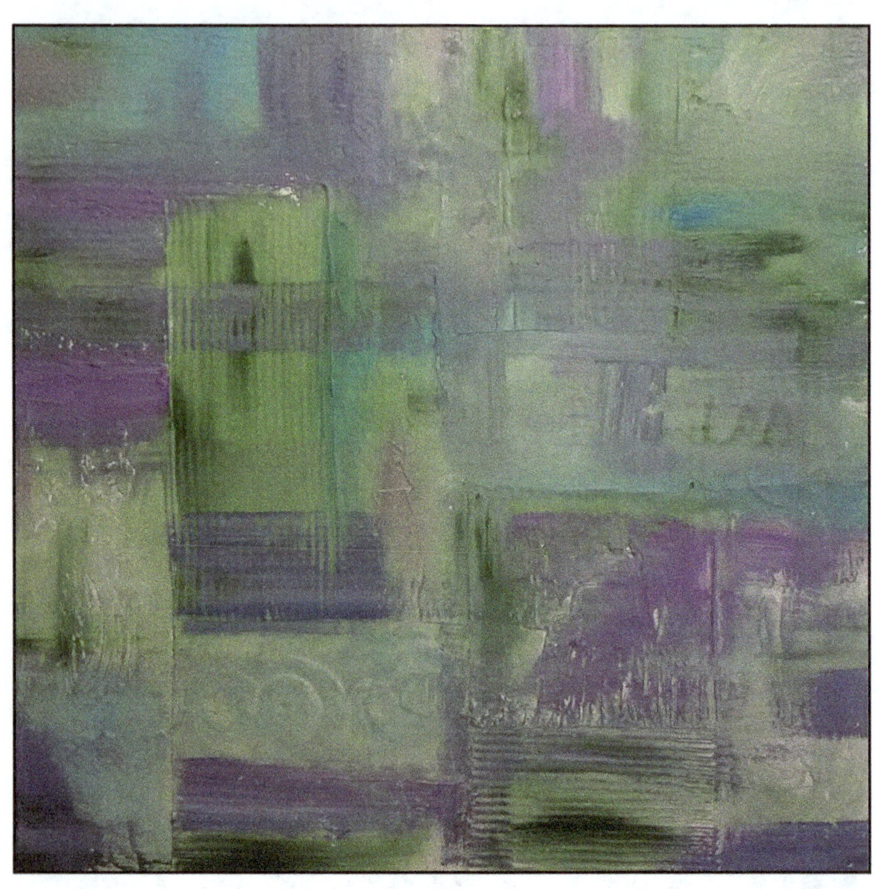

Our Forever Spot

Poured fresh and new
in front of our houses,
the cool gray wetness lay
smooth and perfect,
stretching far away
into the horizon;
at dusk, it still shone
damply beckoning;

we were young,
laughing and carefree,
you said,
let's do our handprints

so we did,
smacking them down
into the gray damp

then you said,
let's do our initials

so we did,
slowly tracing out the letters
with a stick
as if we were kids in school,
practicing
with #2 pencils.

Yesterday
I stood alone
in our forever spot,
even alone I could
hear your laughter echo
through time,
I could
see your eyes glint
across eternity;

I knelt
placing my hands
in your prints,
tracing your initials
with my fingers,

alone
I could look down the sidewalk
stretching
far away
beyond the horizon.

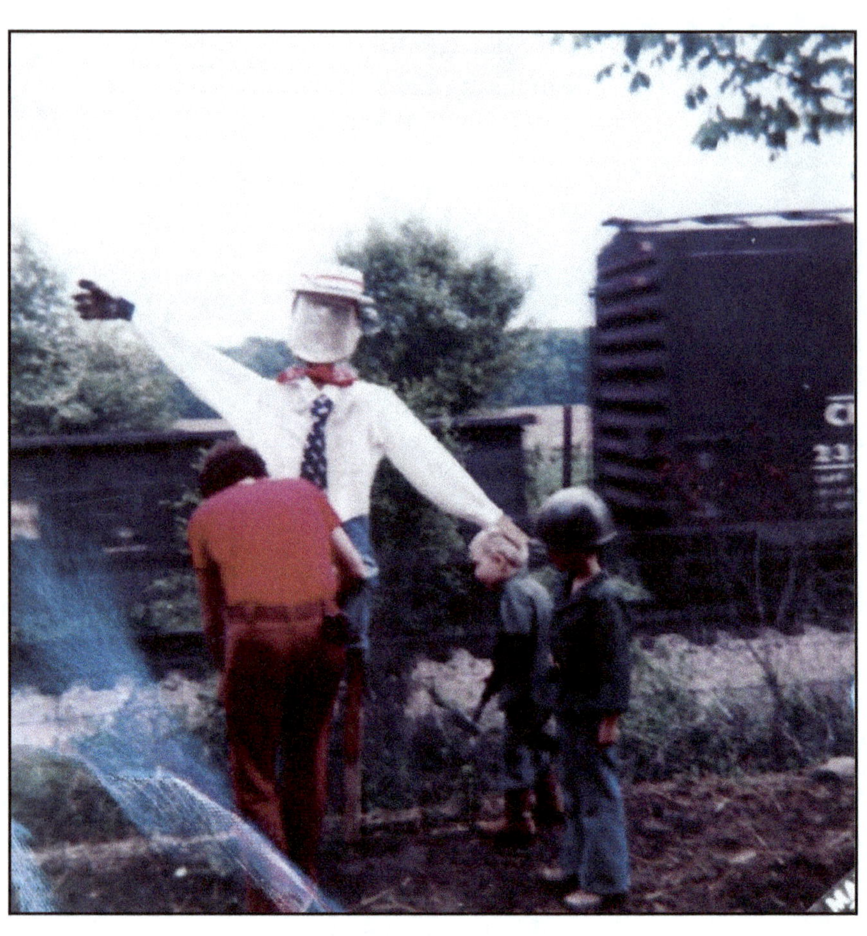

Old Scarecrow Man

Behind our house
~ oh way back when ~
we built us an old Scarecrow Man;
he had one arm up,
flung to the sky,
and a hat we called a porky-pie;
Dad's old white shirt
fit pretty well,
jeans tied on ~ tighter'n hell;
a ragged red bandana
added some flare,
that tie we got from god knows where;

the day we built him
~ oh time did fly ~
and more'n once our train rumbled by.

Friends, I gotta tell ya
right now, today,
as time and dear ones have passed away,
of everything we loved
~ oh way back when ~
like our yard, our forest, our Scarecrow Man,
the thing we loved most,
the thing that was main,
oh how we loved that rumbling old train!

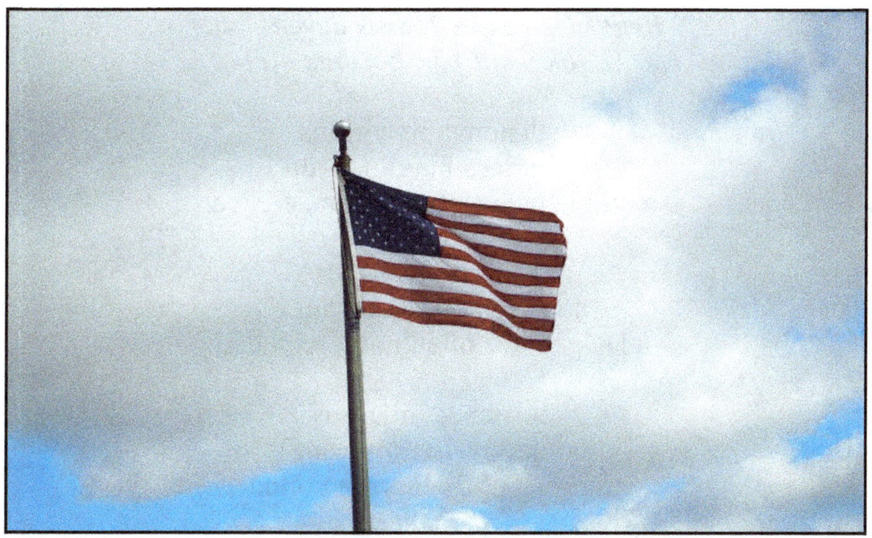

Every Goddamned Day

Well, I wake up early,
with a pretty good feelin',
coffee fills my cup
and my favorite songs are playin'
I poke some paint on canvas,
I hear sweet birds a-singin'
then *ooh* big mistake

I check in online,
one quick look is all it takes
to see the news headlines
~ disasters and alternative fakes ~
they pepper through my feed;

what a world we live in,
our leaders gorged on greed,
but our unconscionable sin
is that we elected them ~
man, whatever happened to
love is all ya need?

Regardez ce que je suis devenu . . .
(*Look what I've become . . .*)

balancing precarious
no fearless Flamingo am I
a one-legged stalwart stand eluded

memory nefarious
no ingenious Tesla am I
a leaky sieve of a brain precluded

existence hilarious
no new *Arlecchino* am I
synapses failing linkage colluded

socially vicarious
no talented Ripley am I
participant observer deluded

revision mysterious
no Eva Jablonka am I
adaptational embrace concluded

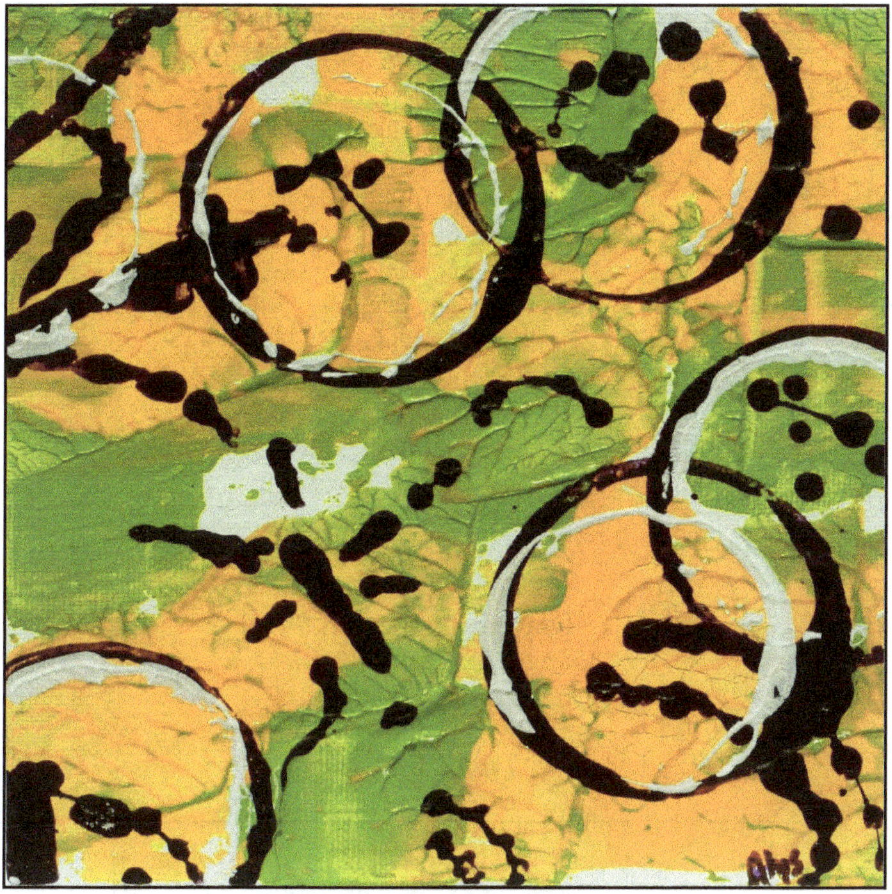

No metaphors, adjectives, adverbs

poem is,
night was,
I sleep.

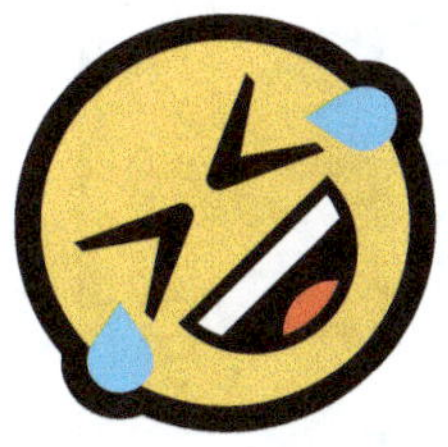
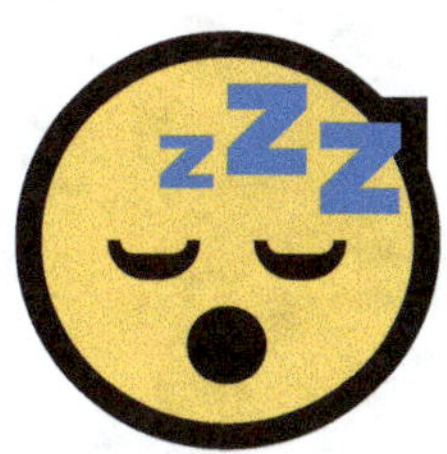

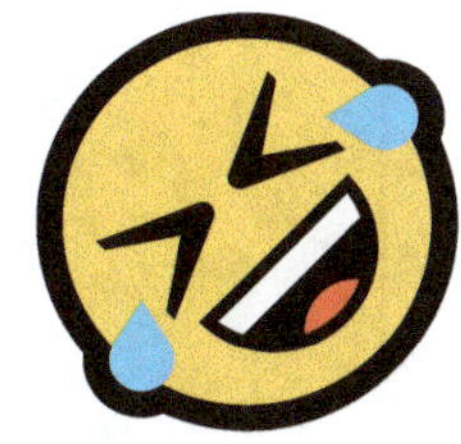

Caol Áit

(*written pre-dawn 08 July 2017, for my mother*)

Awake, awake!
Again and again,
through the mist thick
like an unmindful fog,
a Voice ever fleeting.

Awake, awake!
Unknowing;
always never aware,
of silence's distant echo,
yet ever the Other awaits.

Awake, awake!
O Conjurer!
Draw away the veil,
as in a dream stood still,
temptingly come again.

I am ready.

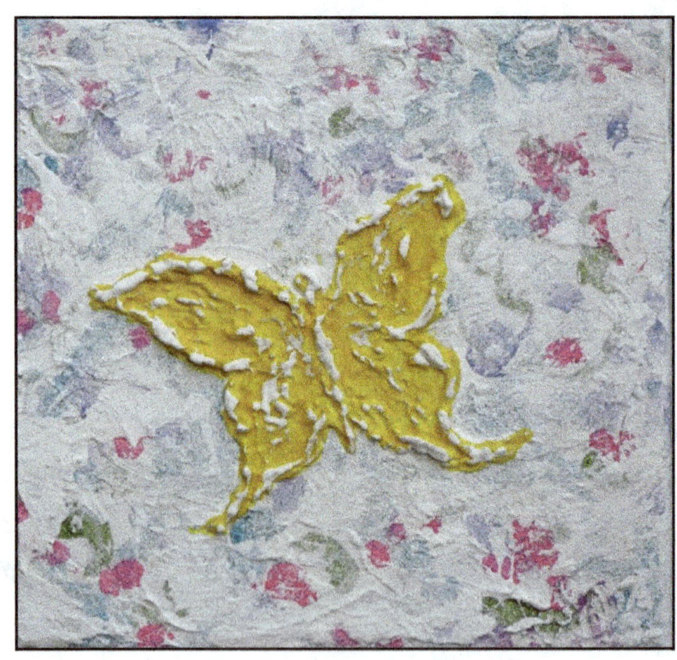

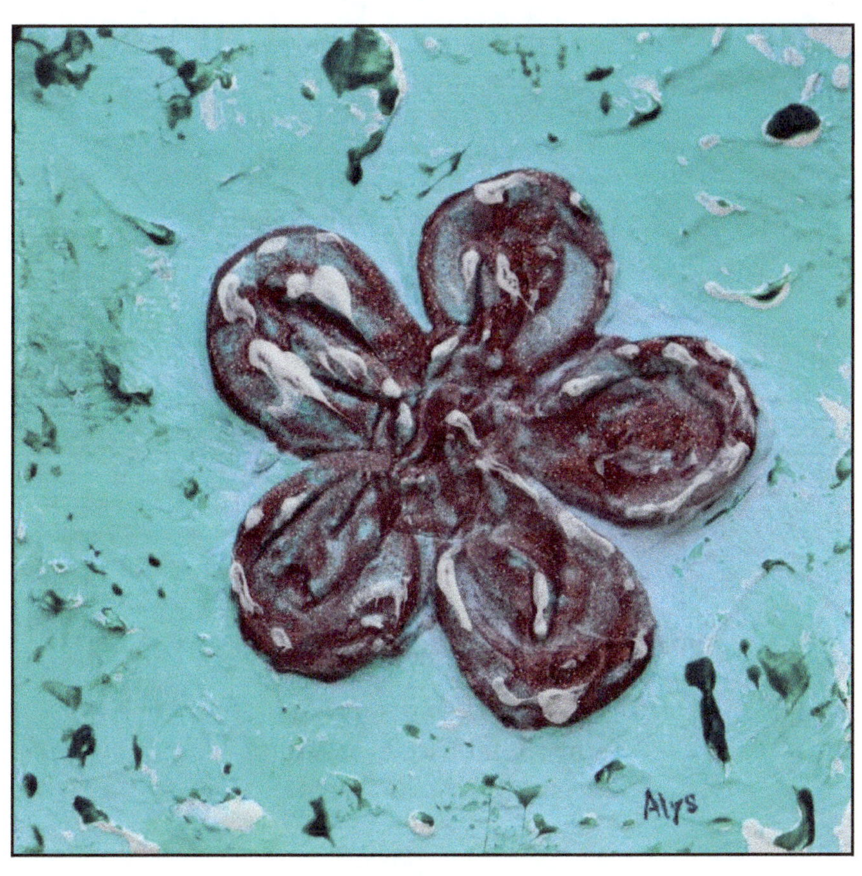

Missing You
(*for Mom,* 01 August 2017)

These days,
there's a bright sun shining
(but not burning),
summer's thick humidity's kept at bay
by sweet breezes blowing puffy white clouds
across a blue blue sky;

I lift my head up
(just like you did)
to feel summer's kiss across my skin;
as the sunlight retires,
descending softly below the horizon,

and soon the stars twinkle and dance
across a midnight sky
and crickets sing their love song,
I close my eyes
(just like you did)
and breath in that soothing lullaby.

These days,
I wander through these rooms,
touching my memories
(just like you did)
my hands glide along the walls,
caressing the years,
marveling that I am in this house
(just like you did);

I lift up my memories
holding in my hand a piece of our history,
turning it over and over,
(like you did)
in my mind I see everything,
every moment shared.

These days,
part of me is you ~
it always was, of course,
but now more than before
I carry you
~ just like you did ~
I remember how you carried your mother
and part of you was her
it always was, of course,
but then even more than before.

These days,
when the sweet breezes blow,
when the happy crickets sing,
when I wander through these rooms,
you are the lighter part of me.

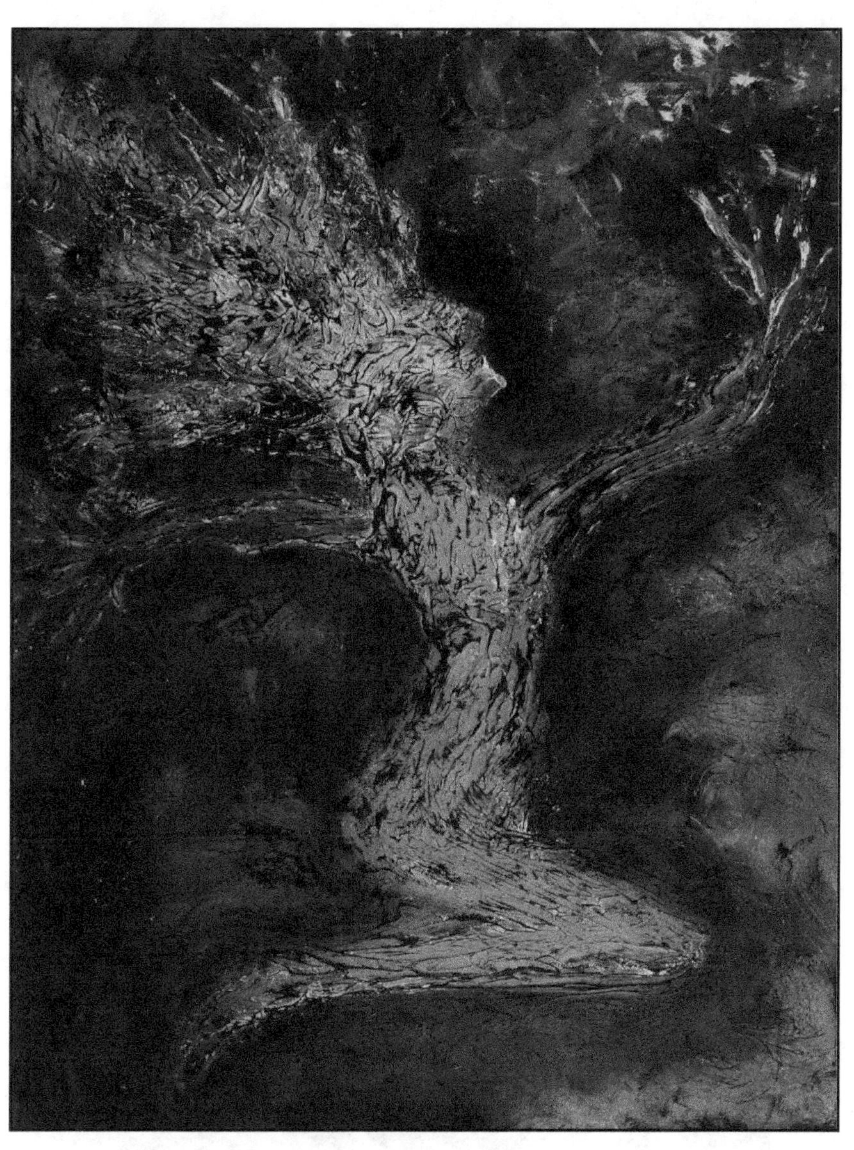

Betrayal

Out of the blue the blow lands
in a heartbeat everything changes
it's like you've been kicked in the stomach
the pain is a blast of red fire in your vision
a numbness in your legs
as you drop to your knees

a white-slash of searing pain
as you gasp for air
that simply isn't there
betrayal comes out of the blue
like a kick in the stomach
and then
you have to stand back up
as sorrow streams out in your tears
and your lungs won't inhale
and your footing is off
and you feel like your heart is fractured
you lurch forward
then step back into the shadows
because you feel
wounded and ashamed
exposed and humiliated
even though you know
you did nothing wrong
betrayal comes out of the blue
like a kick in the stomach

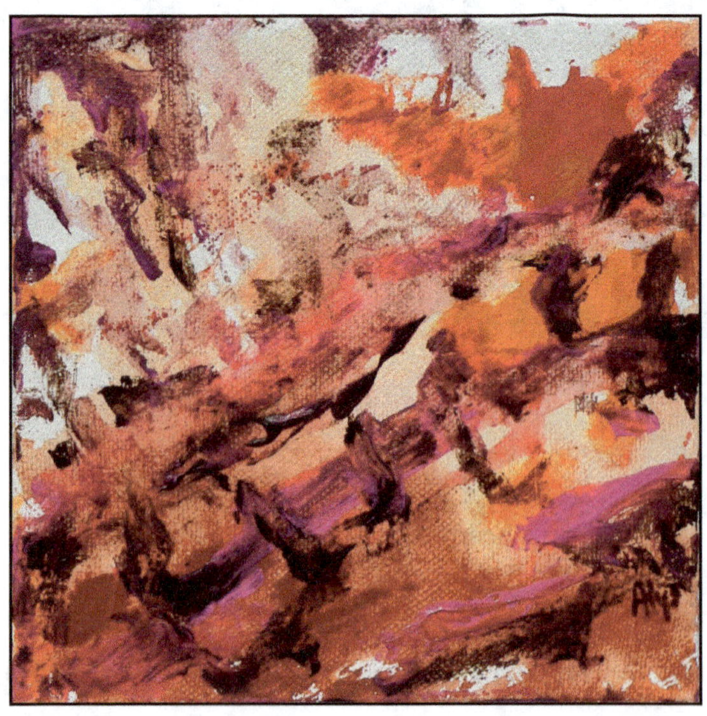

Purplehaired Smartass

(Here's my words to the tune of
Longhaired Redneck by David Allan Coe & Jimmy Rabbit)

Folks 'round here all knows that I'm an ar-teest
But they never buy my paintings in this dive
Where hippies wink at rednecks
who are buying from the bikers
Who are selling shit to anyone left alive

The loudmouth in the corner's gettin' to me
Talking 'bout my clothing and my hair
I guess he ain't read the signs that say I been to college
Someone ought to warn him 'fore I talk him off his chair

'Cuz my purple hair can't cover up my smartass
And I've won every fight I've ever talked
Hey, I don't need some turkey telling me I ain't assimilatin'
'Cuz he don't know the damned ol' battles I fought

'Cuz I can talk rings 'round all y'all dumbasses
And I still mock
all the assholes that I knew
They tell me I look like I'm homeless
And sound like I drink too much Tullamore Dew

And the curator in the last town I exhibited in
Knew the inspiration of every piece I showed
He said online searches turned him on to all my paintings
Just about the time his TV broke

Yeah, Johnny Cash showed up in my creations
Long before millennials stole that goat
I been a purplehaired smartass for so long, I can't remember
And I can quote from every song John Gilmore ever wrote

'Cuz I can talk rings round all y'all dumbasses
And I still mock
all the assholes that I knew
They tell me, I look like I'm homeless
And sound like I drink too much Tullamore Dew

Yeah folks ’round here all knows that I’m an ar-teest
But they never buy my paintings in this dive
Where hippies wink at rednecks
who are buying from the bikers
Who are selling shit to anyone left alive

The loudmouth in the corner’s gettin’ to me
Talking ’bout my clothing and my hair
I guess he ain’t read the signs that say I been to college
Someone ought to warn him
’fore I talk him off his chair . . .

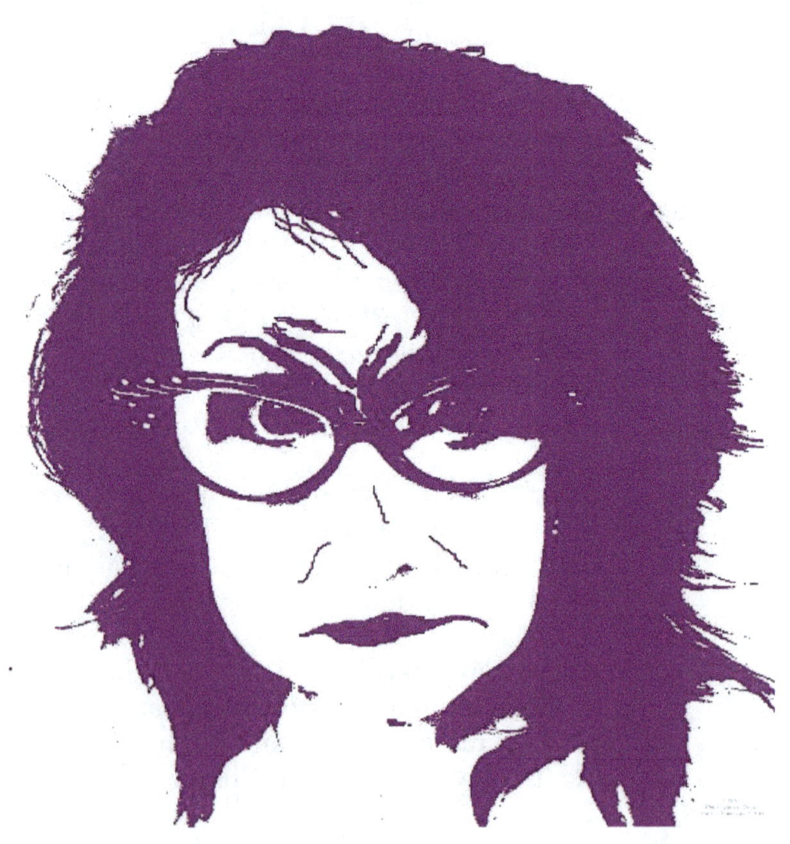

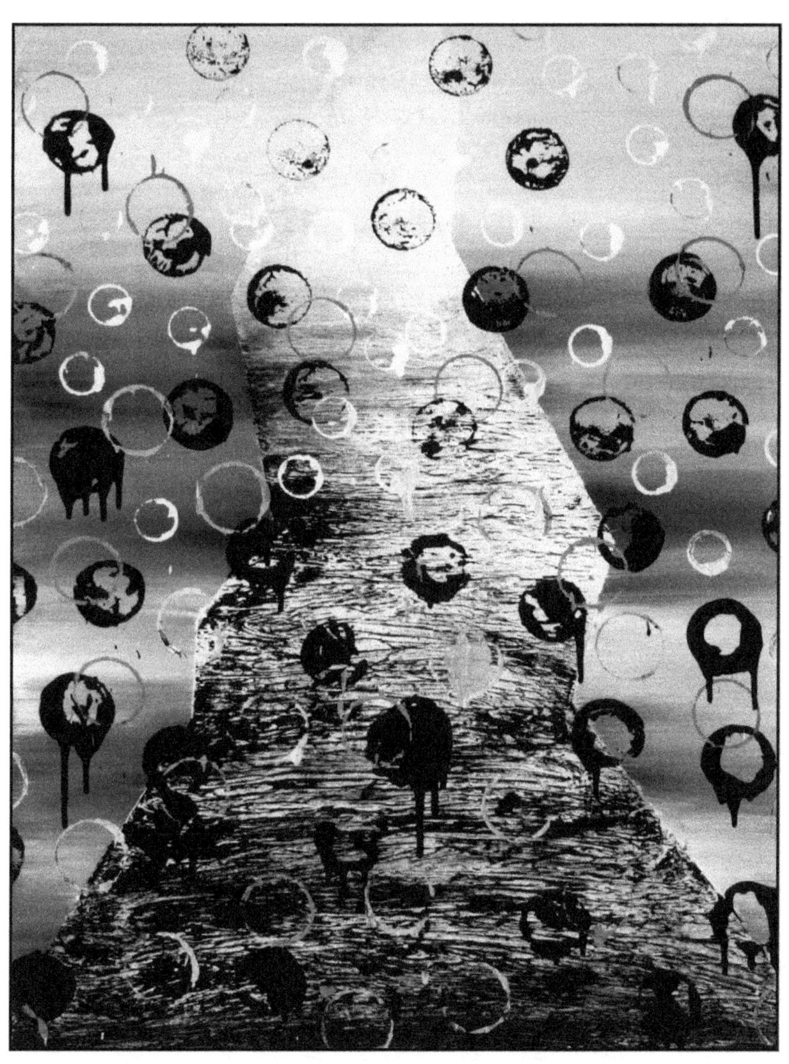

One More Hug

(for my mom, 09 February 2018)

Come again like you did today
wake me
with your sweet voice calling
Alys! Alys! Wake up!
Come again like you did today
in the early hours
when you called me

like you used to do
when it was time to go run
Alys! Alys! Wake up!

Come again like you did today
and I awoke to see you
sitting on my bedside,
I felt the thin pressure of your hip
against my leg
and as you said,
I miss you, Alys

I sat up and wept and cried out
O, I miss you so much, Mom!
then instinctively
reached out to hug you and
felt your flesh warm in my arms,
I felt your bones pressing into me
and smelled your smell
as our heads bowed together
and I clung to you

Then you said,
I know you were always protecting me
and I collapsed inside myself
weeping harder
holding harder onto you
as I felt you fading
and then you said,
Tell Johnny no regrets:
distance never mattered,
he was always with me,
tell him that,
tell him I am with him
forever
and I promised I would,

and then as you faded faded
and I felt your body
dissolving in my arms,
and I tried to hold on,

you said,
Tell Aly to always remember:
she was my magician, my delight
tell her that,
tell her I am with her
forever
and I promised I would

and then desperately I cried,
Mom, don't go, don't go
as you said,
I love you so
and you were gone.

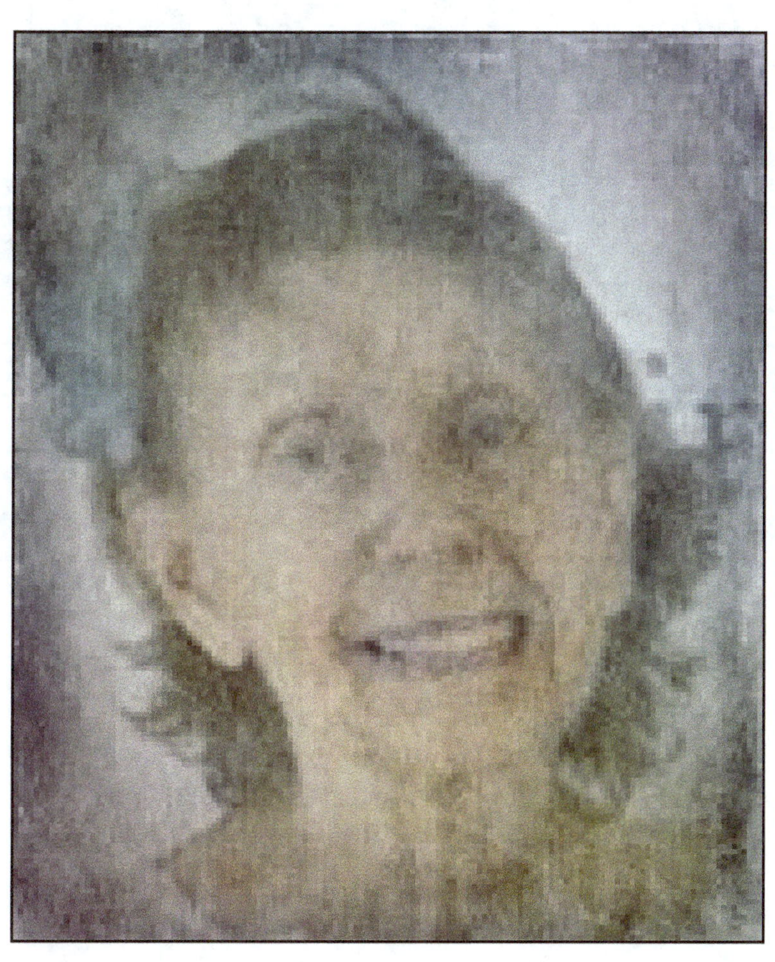

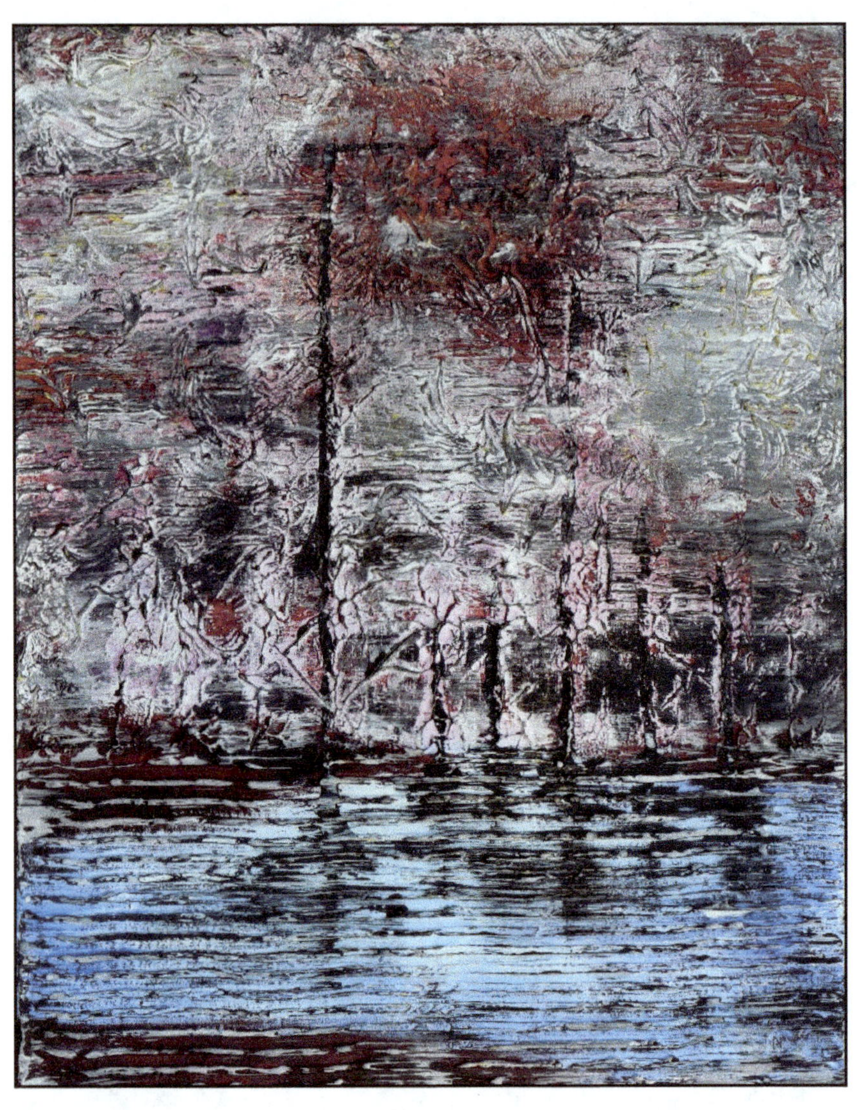

Sailing

I dreamt so oft of his Wine-Dark Sea
so set my Sails aloft,
they shuddered high against Winds and Rains,
whilst I ne'er counted cost,
to me to you to all who knew
the Seas' most mighty Powers;

I cast myself away from all
and turned my face into the lost.

My sailing Ship was tossed and turned, worn
and battled every day,
wearily stood I entrenched at helm
forsworn to never stray,
for me for you for all who knew
the Seas' most mighty powers;
I cast myself into the Breach
and turned up my face in prayer.

No Sun did shine nor did Stars aglow
my journey rattled on,
no Compass led nor strong Oars below
yet steadfast stayed my Sails
for me for you for all who knew
the Seas' most mighty Powers;
I cast myself into their Folds
and turned in my weeping face.

My Sails! My Sails! Aloft e'er were they
through storm and chopping sea,
at weathered helm stood I alone
'twas wings bore Ship and me,
for me or you for all who knew
the Seas' most mighty Powers
I cast myself in the Abyss
and turned up my face with glee.

For does not the Challenge rise our Hearts
for strength 'ere there is none?
Does not the Tumult birth Souls Stalwart
whence Courage needeth run
to me to you to all who knew
the Seas' most mighty Powers?
I cast my Ship into the Storm
and turned my face up to the Sun.

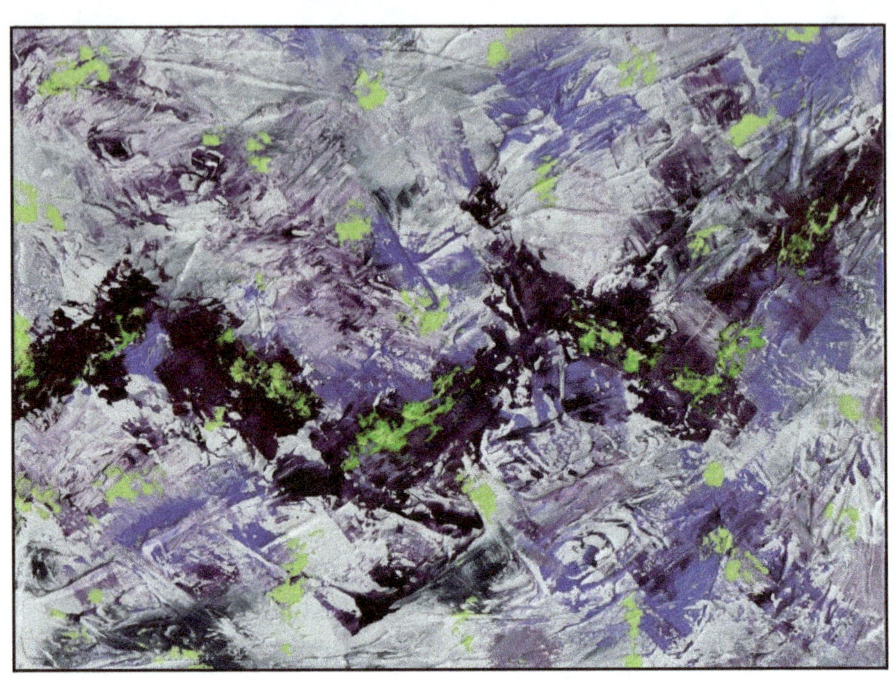

Mother's Day Afternoon

I drank it;
this glass filled to the brim
with fun and food and laughter,
and beloved faces surrounding me,
keeping my sorrow at bay;
this day passed
cradled by love and comfort.

They have gone home,
back to their lives,
the lives they're meant to live,
the lives I painted for them
in my happiest dreams,
and for this moment
sorrow stays in the shadows;
I'm happy here alone.

In my quiet room now
I rest my head upon an old pillow,

as the last sunlight dapples
in painting these walls
with flickering memories old and new;
I watch them, like a favorite film,
knowing you painted this day,
in a dream long ago, for me.

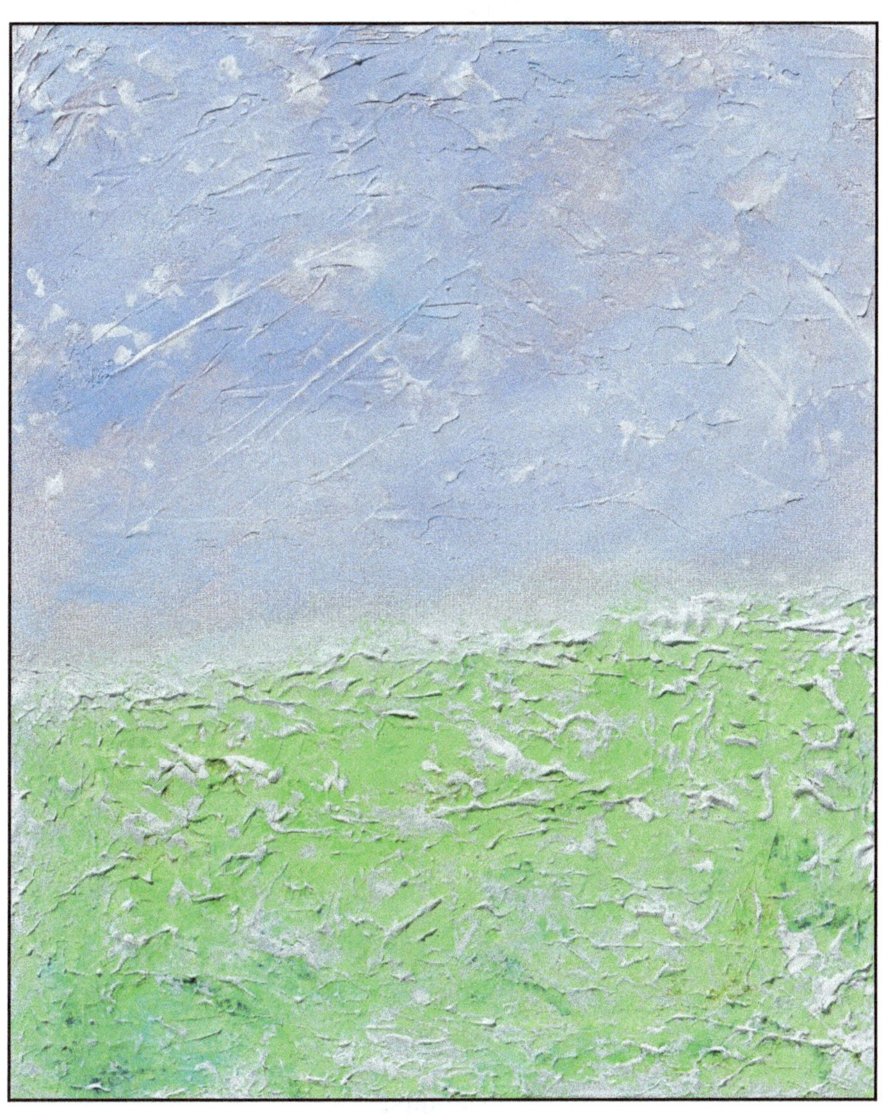

The Pivot

I can't remember not knowing you.

Factually, intellectually, I know
there was a time before we met,
but when was it?
Where is it now?
Time is funky, fluid, eternal.
It folds, it bends, it compresses, it expands,
it's everywhere and in everything
all the time (oh that's *punny*).
I can't see time, but I feel it.
I breath it in, it scrapes through my lungs like a California wildfire.

You're in there somewhere.

Like the fabled mists of time,
meeting you
is so far back in my memory or my consciousness
that I can't find it, I can't see it, I can't feel it;
it is somewhere in a void
of nonexistence that exists forever.
An eternal moment.
I wish it wasn't so.

I wish I could go back to the me that was, before you.
Before *you* in my life.

Now, today, it seems unfair that I can't remember me before you.
I remember so much, why not *that*?

Things I do remember the things you did; they still live within me:
The Slow Isolation.
Cutting Words.
Silences.
Bruises.
Invasion.
Assaults.
(it is still hard to say the word *rape*)

Destruction.
Fires burning my treasures.
Fractures.
Broken teeth.
Fear.
Soul Annihilation.

I also remember what I did:
Hurt.
Cry alone.
Never tell.
Exist in fear.
(not "live in fear": there was no living)
and then
Escape.
(that was *The Pivot*)
It took a long time to get away.
I had nothing. I had nowhere. I went anyway.
It was go . . . or die.

They call it *recovery*, I guess, or *PTSD*.
Although *PTSD* is ongoing, so maybe that dark downward time trying to climb up back to something that felt like *me* wasn't PTSD but rather something else. Maybe *recovery*. But *recovery* associates with *addiction*, right? I wasn't addicted to you.
I was imprisoned *by you.*
I escaped.
(that was *The Pivot*)

The Pivot took me down down down into a darkness unimaginable and also lost in the mists of time.

When I turned away from you, I faced that darkness.
I turned away from you to save myself.
Or rather, what was left of my *self.*
I had to face such bleakness.
Processing, they call it.
I call it staring stoically into the face of *it*.

Staring into the face of *me*
~ of the me I had become ~

facing the grief for the me I had lost,
facing of the fear of the me that was yet to be.

I'm not sure what to call the time after *The Pivot*, after my escape:
maybe even that time, that part of my life,
is so fluid, so funky, so eternal
it is still here now within me.

Still now today, that dark journey folds, it bends,
it compresses, it expands, it's everywhere and in everything all the time.

Because even *Escape* never ends.

Each day when I awaken,
you're with me.

As I walk these halls, as I drive these roads,
as I see and greet and talk
to familiar friendly faces,
you're with me.

As I lay down my head at night,
you're with me.

Always
in my dreaming
and my nightmares,
you're with me.

I wish I could remember
not knowing you.

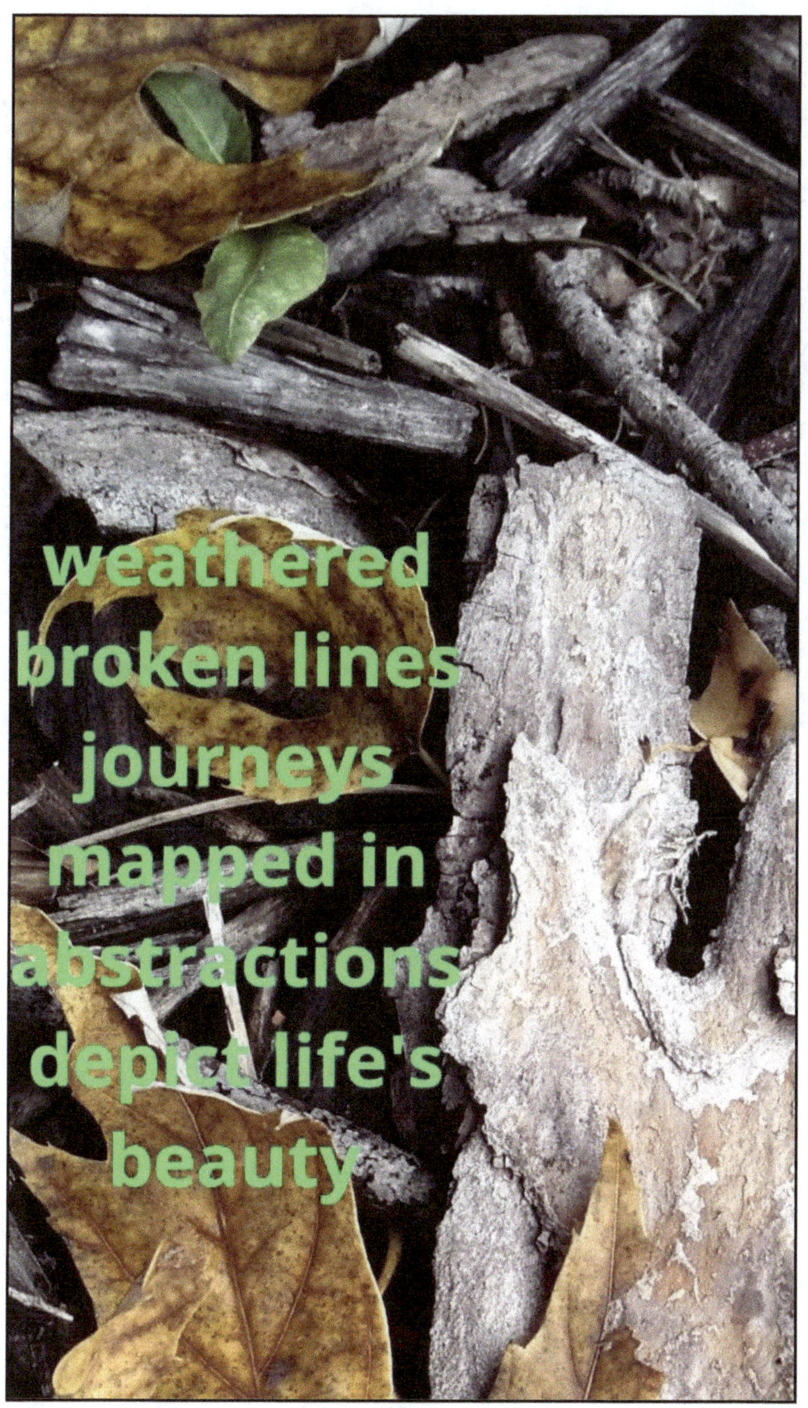
weathered
broken lines
journeys
mapped in
abstractions
depict life's
beauty

Instapoem I

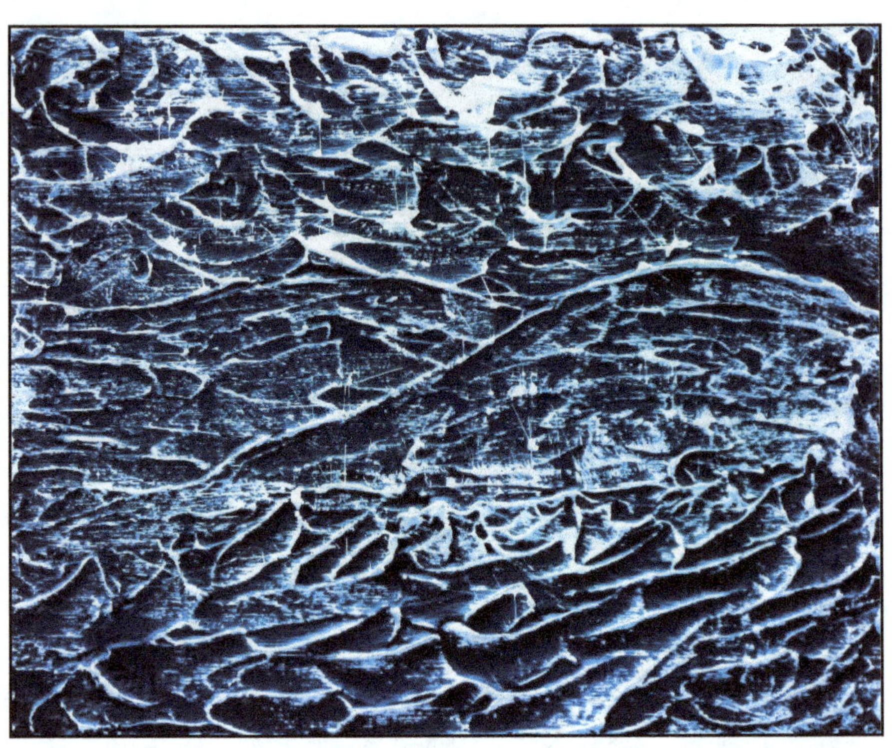

The Good, The Bad, and The But I Don't Wanna

~ The Good ~

Blooming roses in the Spring
and a yellow butterfly dancing
to the tune of bird songs
all summer long
leaves whispering in the trees
then falling gently in the Fall
amidst the still-soft kisses of the wind
poems that come complete
composed in Latin in my mind
as I sleep and when awake
once translated still works
paintings that appear on canvas
as if by magic the layers of my visions
recognizable

Books that read me to sleep
and stay forever in my dreams
movies that pierce my heart
with joy or aching everlasting
beloved faces smiling talking
or just sitting silently here
at our table and
in my memories

~ The Bad ~

Numbed moments and lost days
without ease or kindness
feverish ruminations running
within fevers that run too often too high
Pain thundering on in
oppressive iron weights
upon my chest

Forgotten words and names
elusively flit at the edges
of this leaky sieve of a brain
take a breath
(will the word come through this time?)
When “the first one” means
there’s more and
despairing after each

Off balance
knocking over and into
everything peripheral
coffee spills regularly
as my hand hits my cup
I really do walk into doors
and cupboards and even walls

~ The But I Don’t Wanna ~

get up
pay attention
do laundry

clean (anything)
cook (anything)
see (anyone)
go (anywhere)
think
speak
move
or wear
real clothes
cuz my ‘merz
(flannel shirts & pajama pants)
are so damn comfy

The *but I don't wanna* days
slip in quietly
like a cat burglar
but the aftermath is
total devastation
irreplaceable items
(my precious stolen days)
a hurricane's destruction
the *but I don't wanna* days
live in the Eye of a Storm

Covenant

Chosen,
she stands stoic
unable to turn or look away.

She is bound;
victim and witness
to his destruction and his promise.

Their bond
stands stoic and eternal,
a covenant of love.

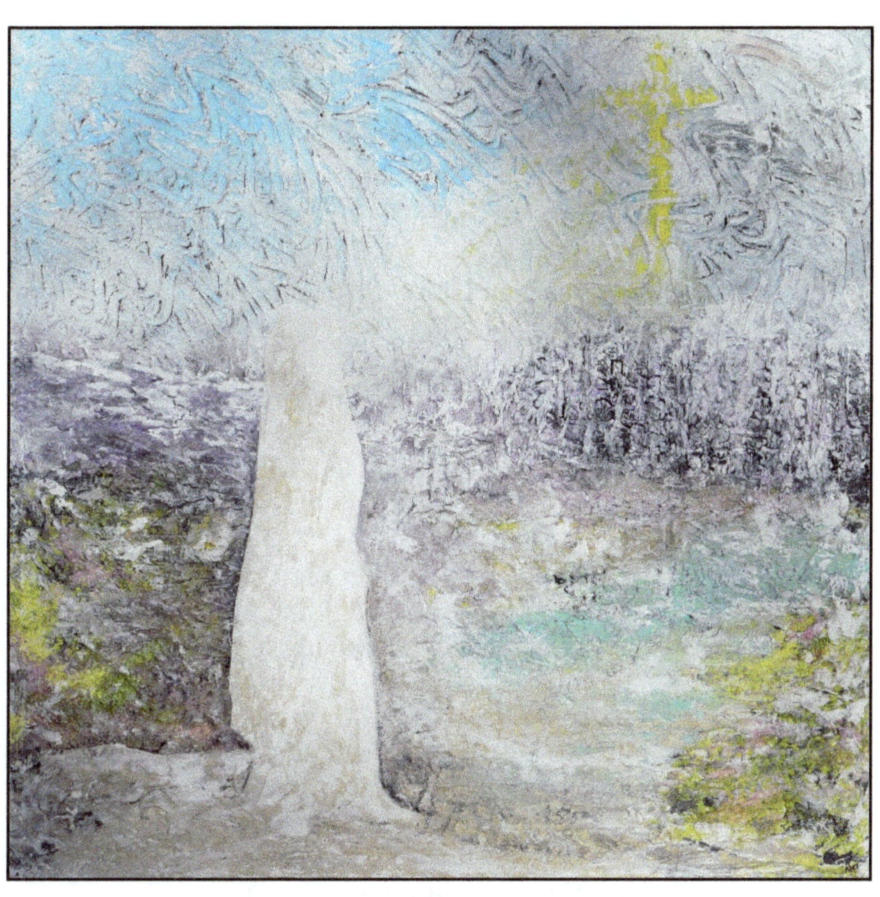

Witness

(*haiku*)

fiery lightning strikes
absolute devastation
salt tears eternal

Dawn

Dawn is daily born
in a myriad of yellows and peaches
and pinks and lavenders;
her colors slide up into the dark night's sky

with both form and function,
purpose and ease.

Her colors, I said,
because she seems to be a woman,
at least by our ridiculous culturally-defined
gender-related color norms
following ancient Greco-Roman tradition.

In the Spring,
she springs up bursting with energetic frenzy,
sweeping away the pre-sunrise fogs
and the dying Winter's last clouds
as if she carries before her a witch's broom.

Her awakening on a Summer morn is slow,
she stretches out her long warm wiggling golden fingers
as if to tickle away the dank and cloying humid night air.

Her spirit wanes a bit in the Fall,
and she awakes with a cool sigh,
knowing her strength,
like that of our older selves,
is starting to fade;
her colors are a little less intense,
her reach into the dark sky is a little less far.

She yawns most sleepily at daybreak in Winter.
Like the rest of us unwilling to arise
into the cold dark air,
she resists leaving the warm confines
of her bedding among the nighttime stars.

Dawn is daily born;
she is like a magician,
waving across our world her magical scarves
of ever-changing tints and shades
and tones of pinks and yellows
and peaches and lavenders.

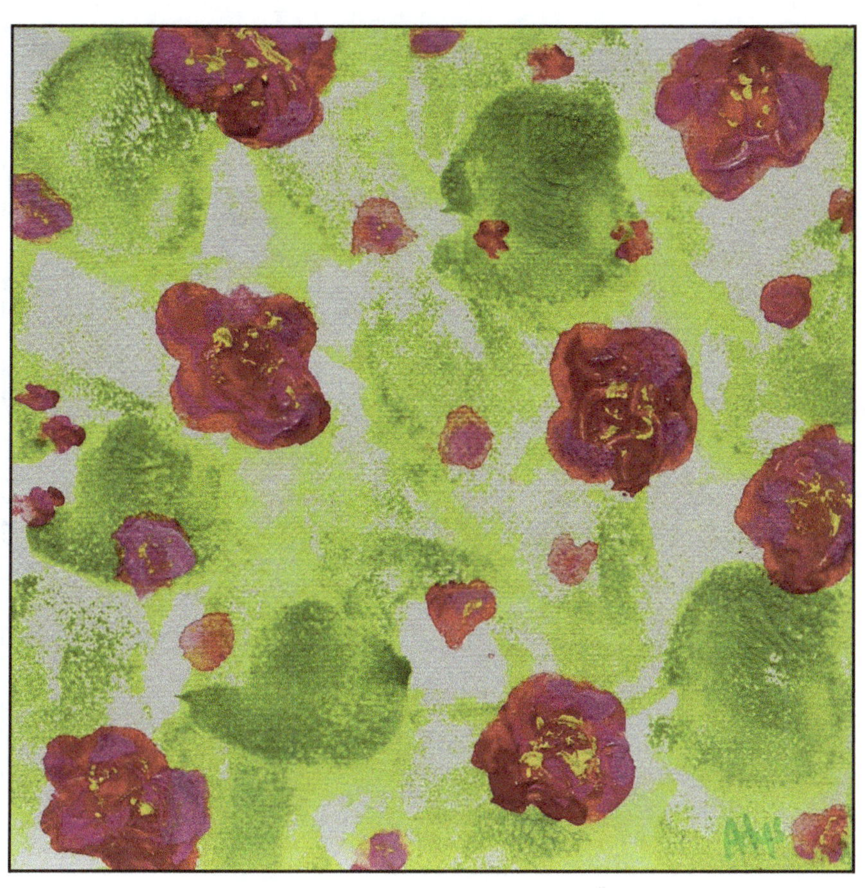

Riding Out The Storm

soft raindrops fall from amethyst clouds
misty and sweet
they slowly build falling
harder and faster
until a sheet of water
cascades and floods like a waterfall
or a solid screen
shielding everything
except the birds
who hide under amber leaves
riding out the storm

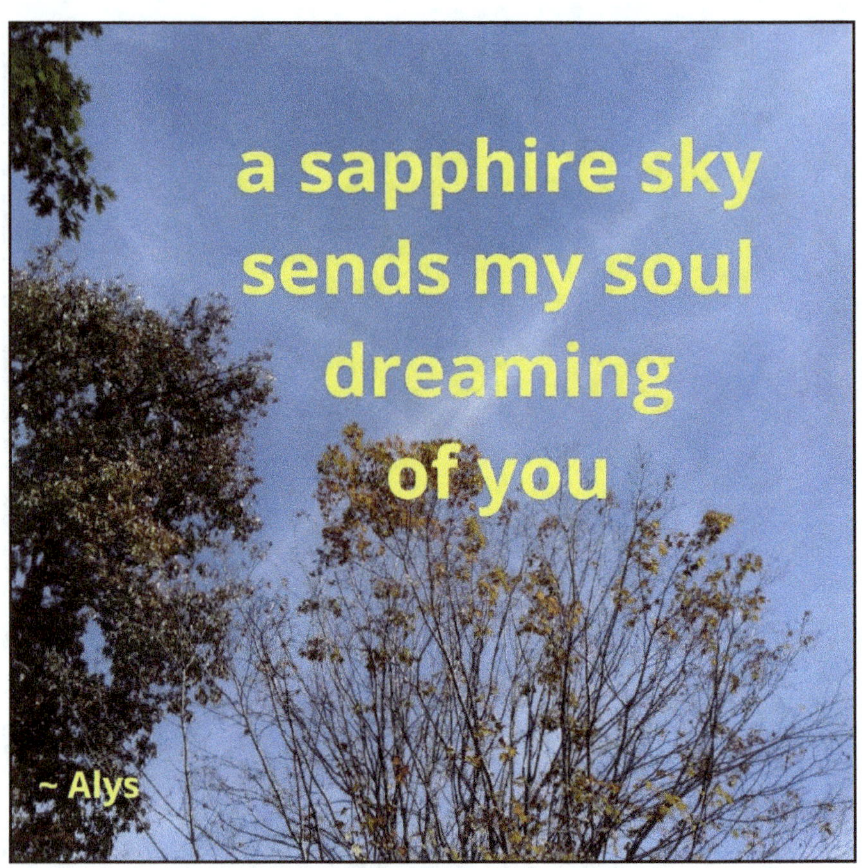

Instapoem II

Remembering

sometimes
like a sudden breeze
across my face
or bright sunlight
revealed by drifting clouds
memories of you
come unbidden

Memory

Her downward gaze
belied
the superiority
of her spirit.

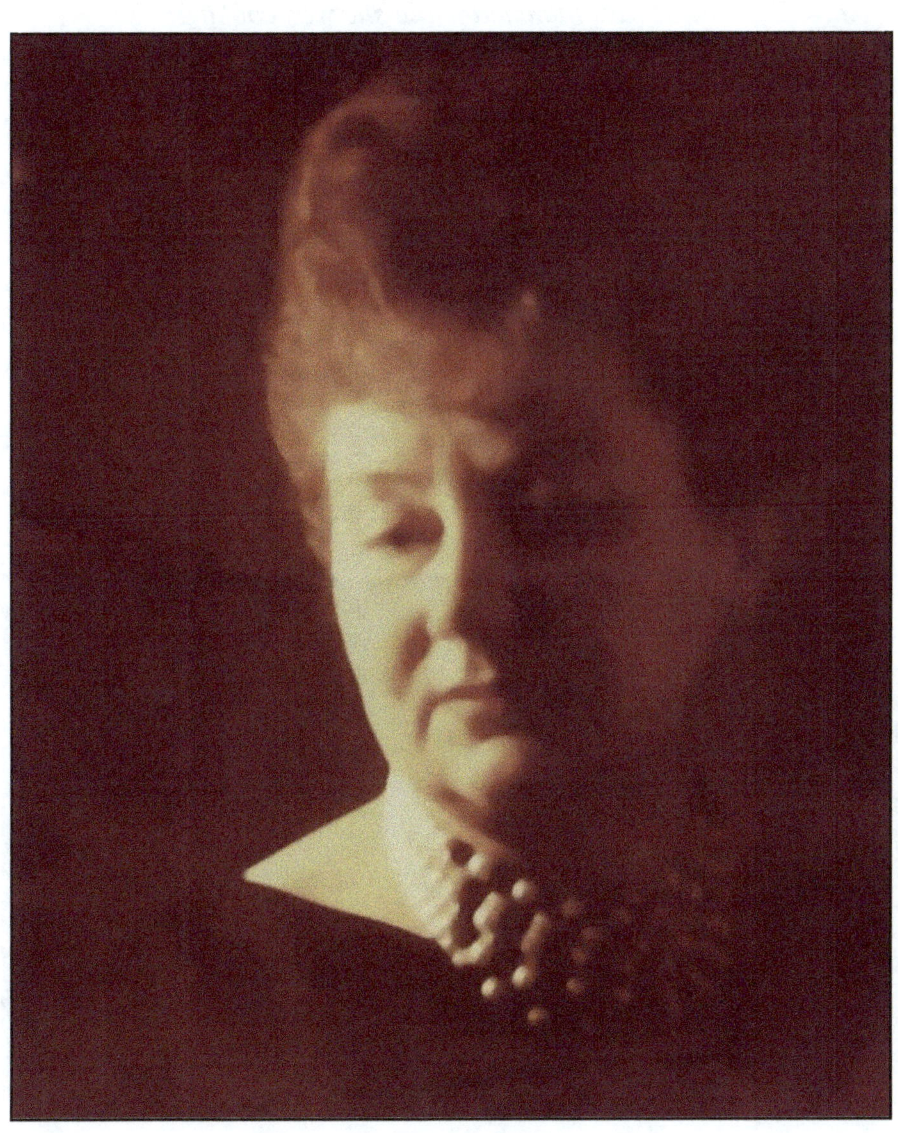

Awash

In her kitchen, my mom smiled at me
as I was cooking for us and I said,
whatchu smiling at?

She said,
You are just like your Grandmommy Alys.
She always hummed while she was cooking;
she always hummed while doing things with her hands.
You do that, too,
when you work with your hands.
You are just like her.

My Grandmommy Alys
for whom I was named
was my first love, my *Dearest* with a capital *D*.
I had no idea that I hum
whilst working with my hands
cooking
painting
doing my projects
but now I hear myself
humming Grandmommy's tune
and I see my mom's smile.

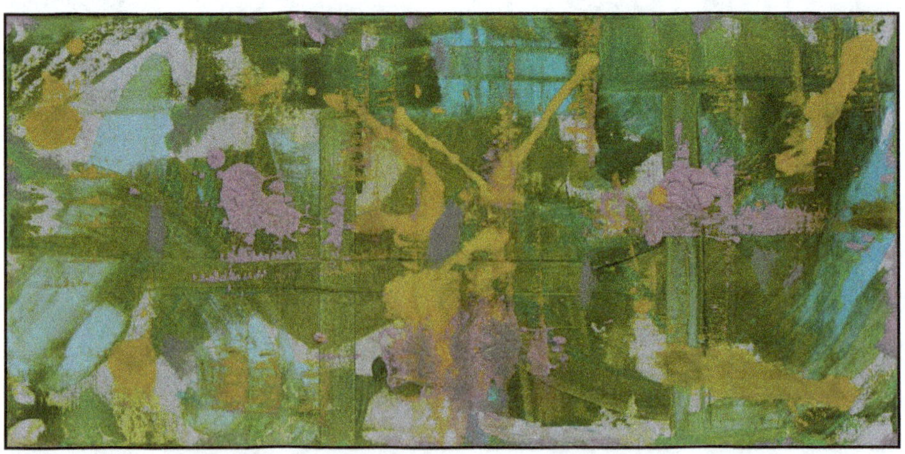

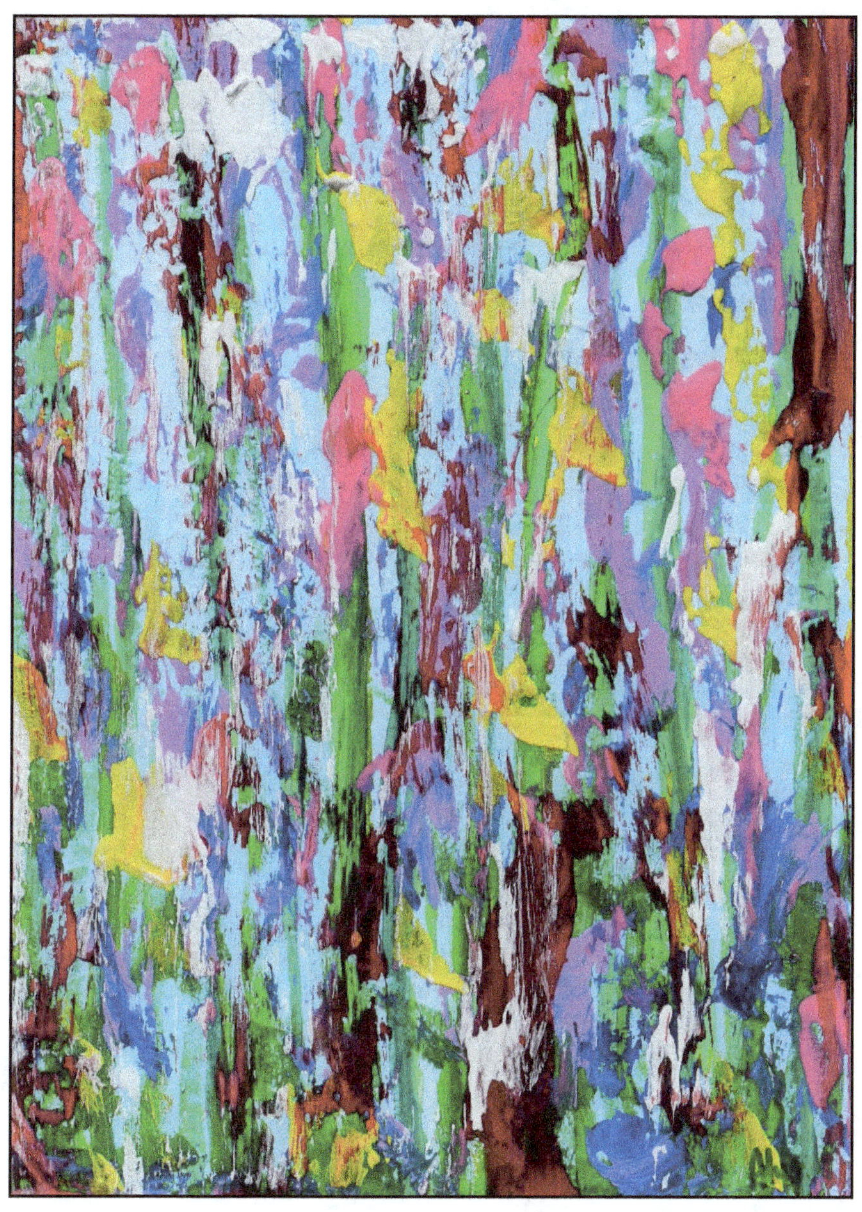

Indiana Spring

Dawn comes cold;
Winter's grip tightly
clutches his ragged-shawl edges,
his furious bellowing

now muted
to silent gasps of chilly air
that feel like light slaps
from an old indignant man
weakened by time.

He has no power, no strength;
he can't withstand
the glory
of the Valkyrie
galloping in,
sword flashing
rainbows of light
infusing clouds and skies
wings whooshing warmth
blowing away
Old Man Winter's
cobwebbed remains.

By midday, he gasps his last;
silently he slinks away
pulling his ragged-shawl edges close,
shivering in his weakness
snarling inside
already plotting
the distant dream
of his return
but
until that cold day dawns
she is victorious.

February birthday haiku

pink and orange sky
delivering Spring's first kiss
morning diamonds shine

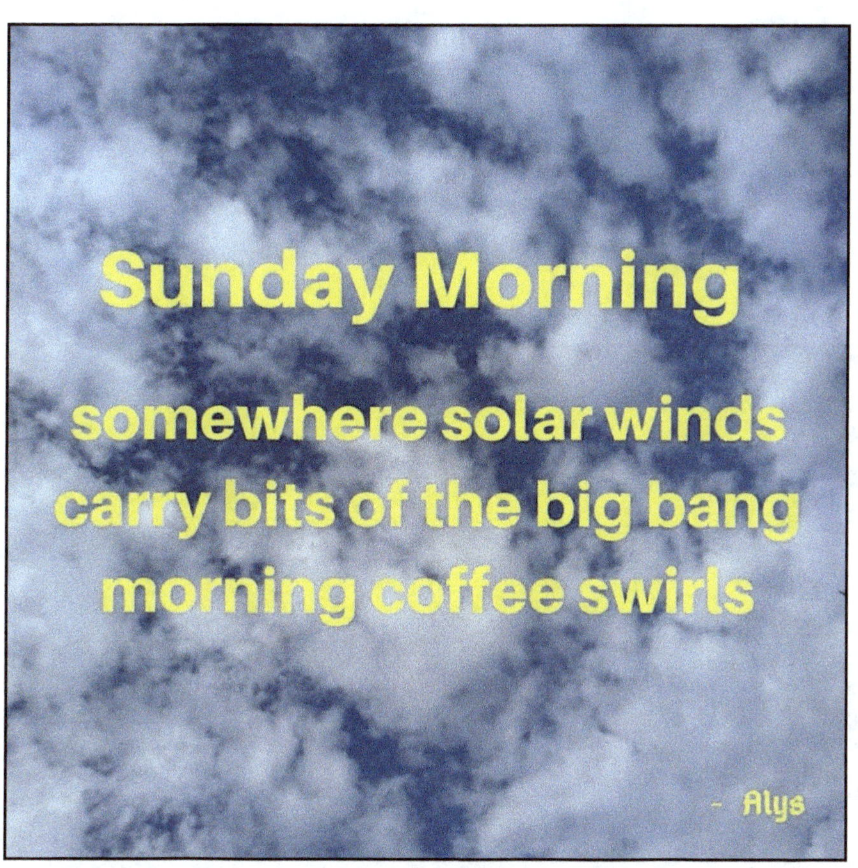

Instapoem III

The Gift

Unexpectedly
it appeared

in splendor
there among the detritus

like a sunrise
on a Summer morning

moving with a softness
unhurried

sanding down
the dangerous edges

the sharp wreckage
of my life.

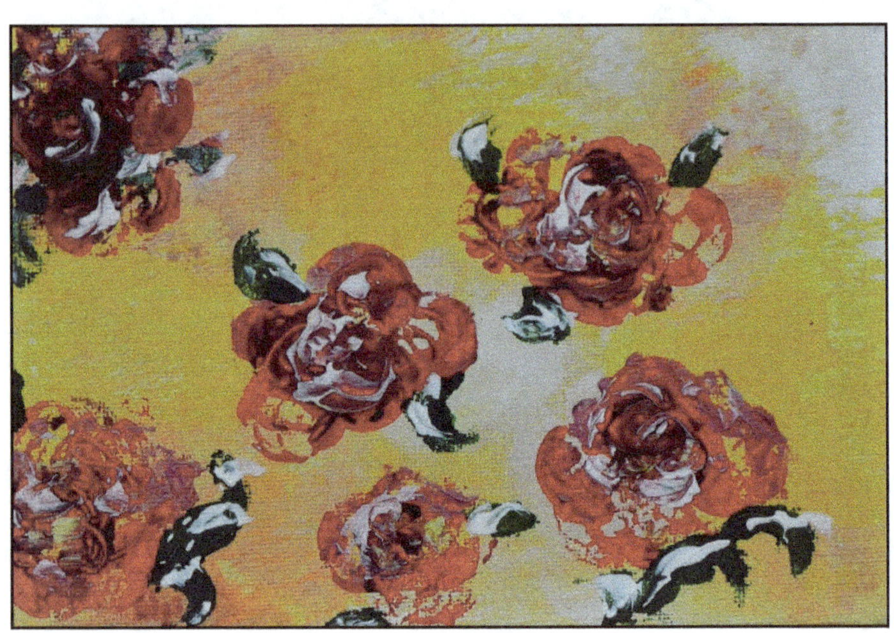

Flowers Die

Blooming,
they intoxicate with
sensations so sweet.

Fading,
they dismay with
sensations of decay.

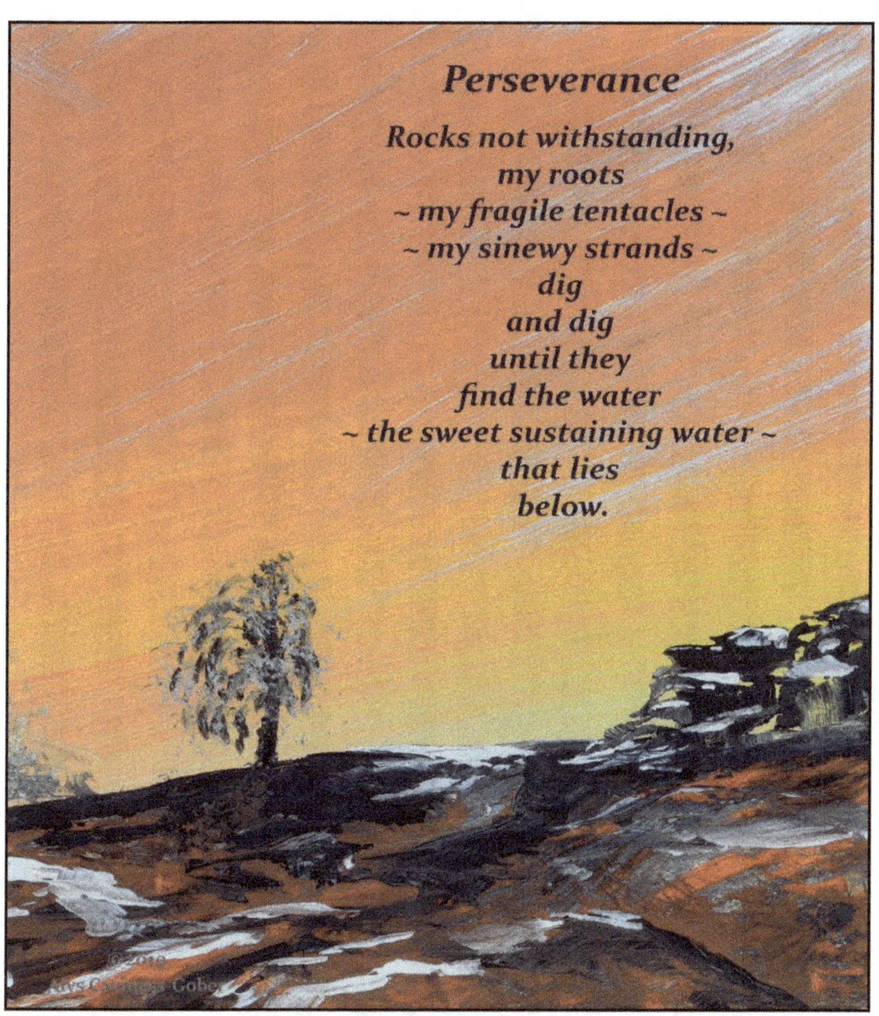

Instapoem IV Perseverance

Solitude

Seeing them
amongst crowds
worlds turning
lives burning
feels like solitude

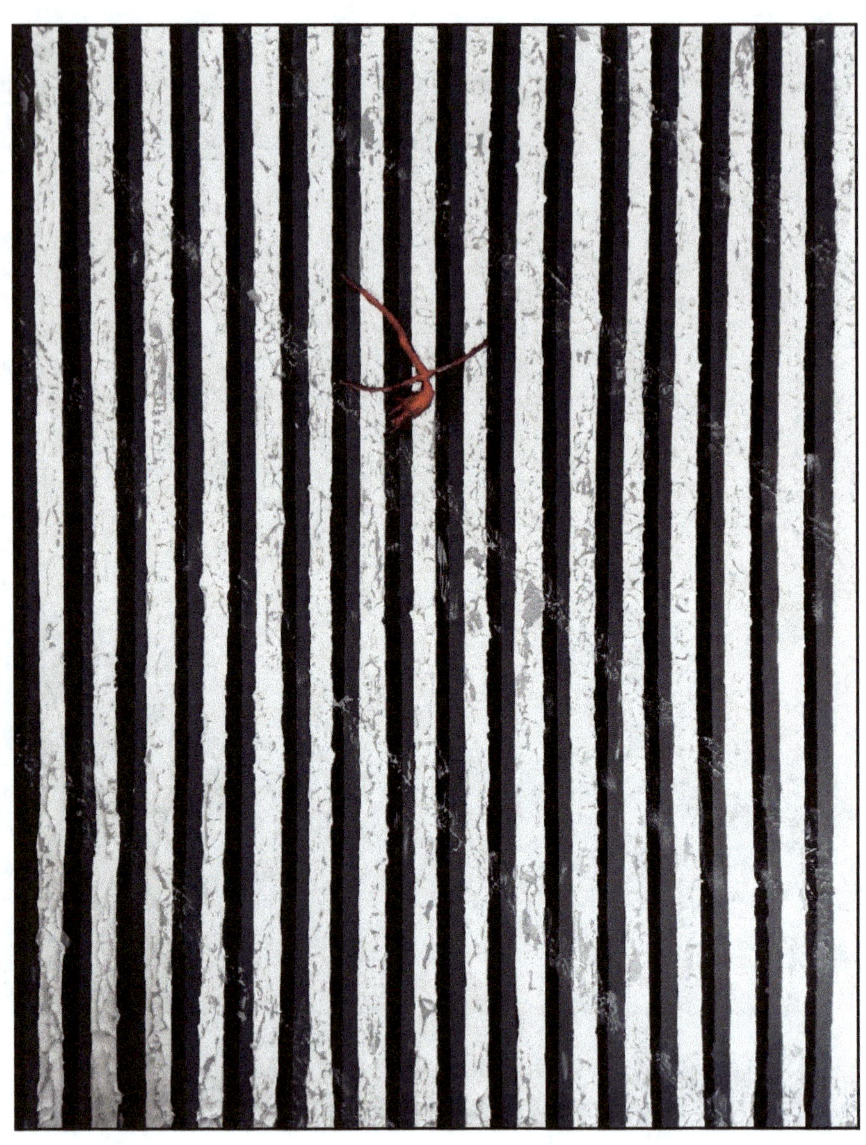

Lady In Red

the image of
the lady in red
against black and gray and white stripes ~
the steel and concrete and glass of the tower ~
proved my remoteness from her reality

in a split second
on my TV screen
she was forever seared into my soul
burned into the retina of my mind's eye
she was frozen forever in time

the fall was for her a lifetime
as her red dress cocooned her
in that moment I couldn't tell
where it ended and her hair began
flowing out as she fell

(*what would I have done?*)

is it wrong that I felt connected?
I wasn't there
I wasn't hurt
I lost no one
the tragedy
wasn't mine
I just watched as
some part of me fell down with her
some part of her fell into my heart

the decades since echo within
requiring a reconciliation

we are threads entwined
the fabric of humanity cannot be rent
she is a thread that weaves through me
seamlessly becoming forever frozen like Lot's Wife
witness eternal
she is all of them
she is all of us
I bear her presence
for I am their
witness eternal

For Luke

One bright Spring day
on a songbird's wings
across a golden sky
with your sweet *Godzirah* kisses
you flew into our hearts
nestling in
forever.

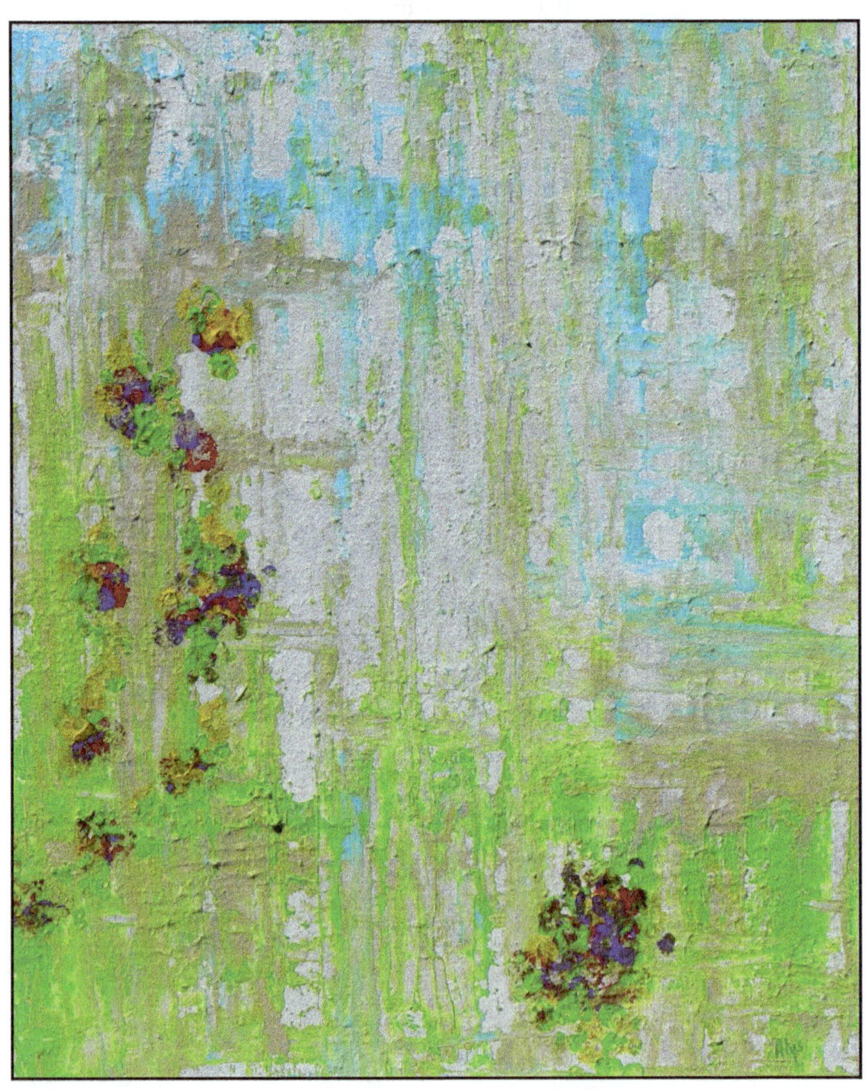

Ancestry Remembers (Now I Am Baba)

Ancestry remembers all of them,
the ones who came before,
the ones I know and remember,
the ones I cannot recall
or never even knew,
and now
I stand with them forever;
because of you,
now I am *Baba*.

The Magick Boy

(*my nonny-nonny song for Luke*)

There was a boy
a Magick Boy,
he loved to laugh
and sing his songs;

he'd sing his songs
and everyone
would dance along
when the Magick Boy
would sing his songs

There was a boy
a Magick Boy,
he loved to laugh
and sing his songs;

he'd sing his songs
and everyone
would dance along
when the Magick Boy
would sing his songs

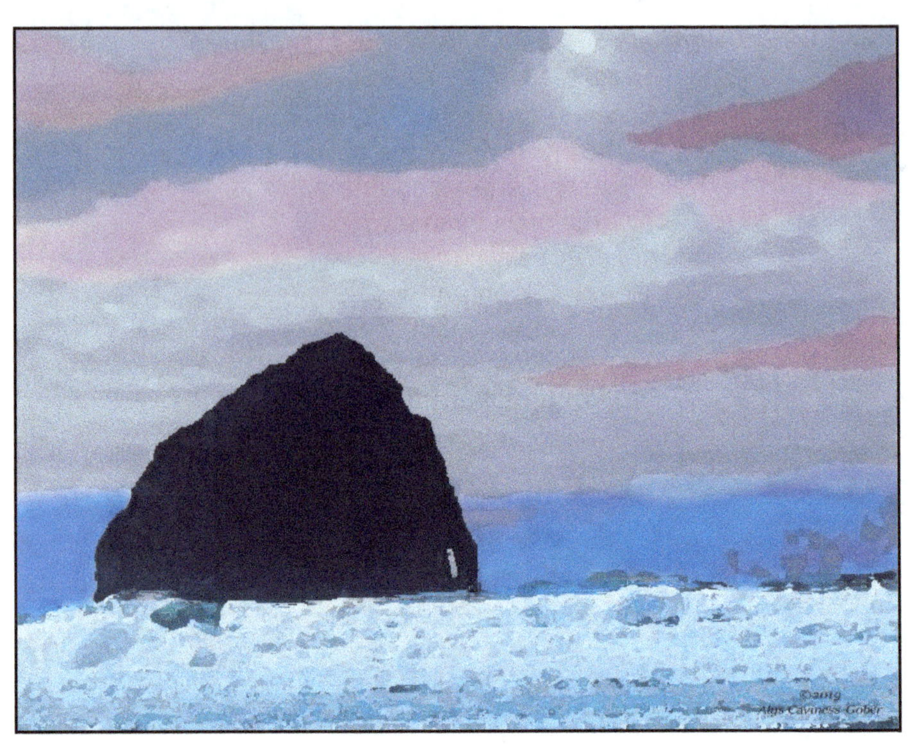

Grief

I remember . . .
standing in wet sand
at the edge of my world
as the cold fingers
of the crashing Pacific
flicked across my toes
and flayed the bare skin
of my feet and
encircled my ankles
freezing my blood and bones
as the sand
shifted
beneath me
and I almost lost
my balance.

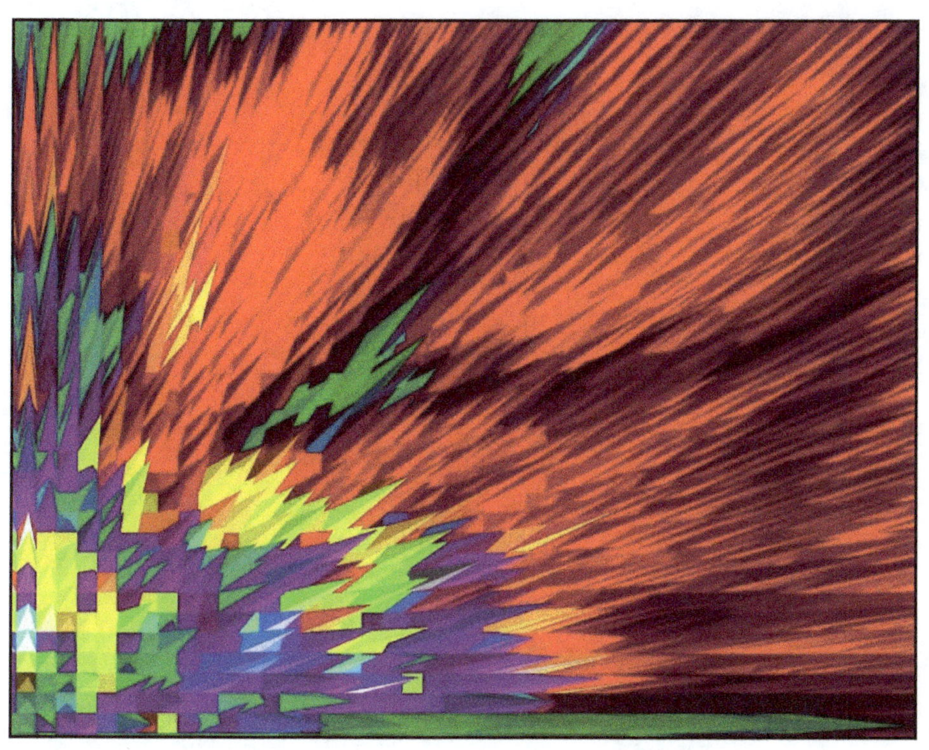

Miles And Miles

I awoke in tears
hearing my father's voice,
remembering . . .

Miles and miles
through the cold and ice
of frozen tundras,
miles and miles
running fevered
on hot shimmering roads,
miles and miles
in dark shadows
of lost forests;

miles and miles
forsaken

miles and miles
through sunlight
so bright
stabbing my heart
with pure joy,
miles and miles
of dancing along
starlit paths,
miles and miles
encircled by and
encircling love

miles and miles
hiding away
inside myself,
miles and miles
of distance
between us,
miles and miles
of reaching

miles and miles
running away,
running towards,
running into,
running out of,
just running

I've run
miles and miles
carrying so much
fear
grief
joy
luck
and always
love

Summer's Remembrance
(haiku)

summer's remembrance
echoing in your heartbeat
a rosebud remains

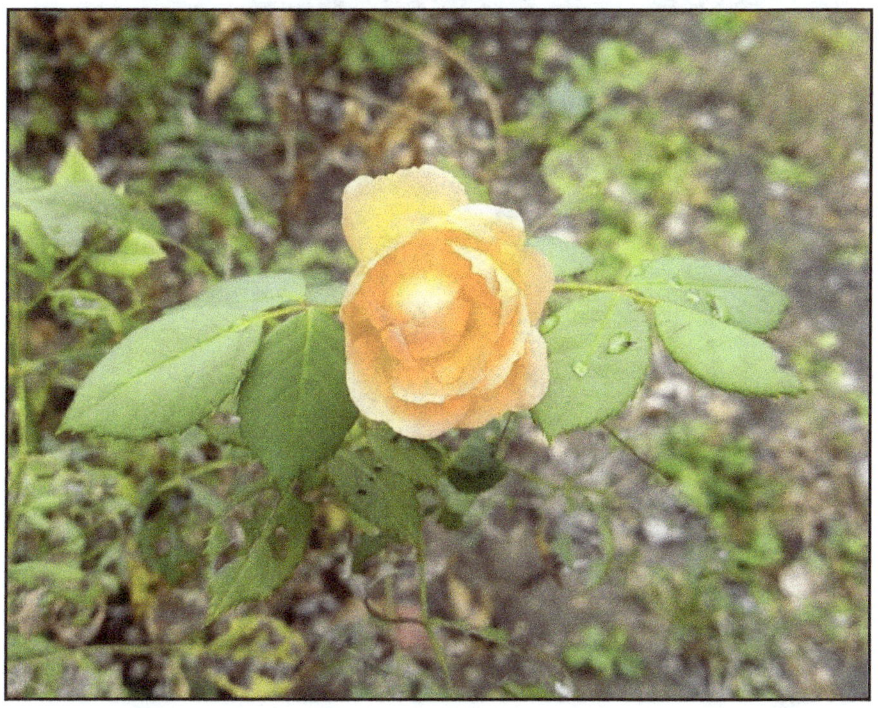

Long Past

overhead starlight shimmers
as far off thunder crashes
they dance through the night

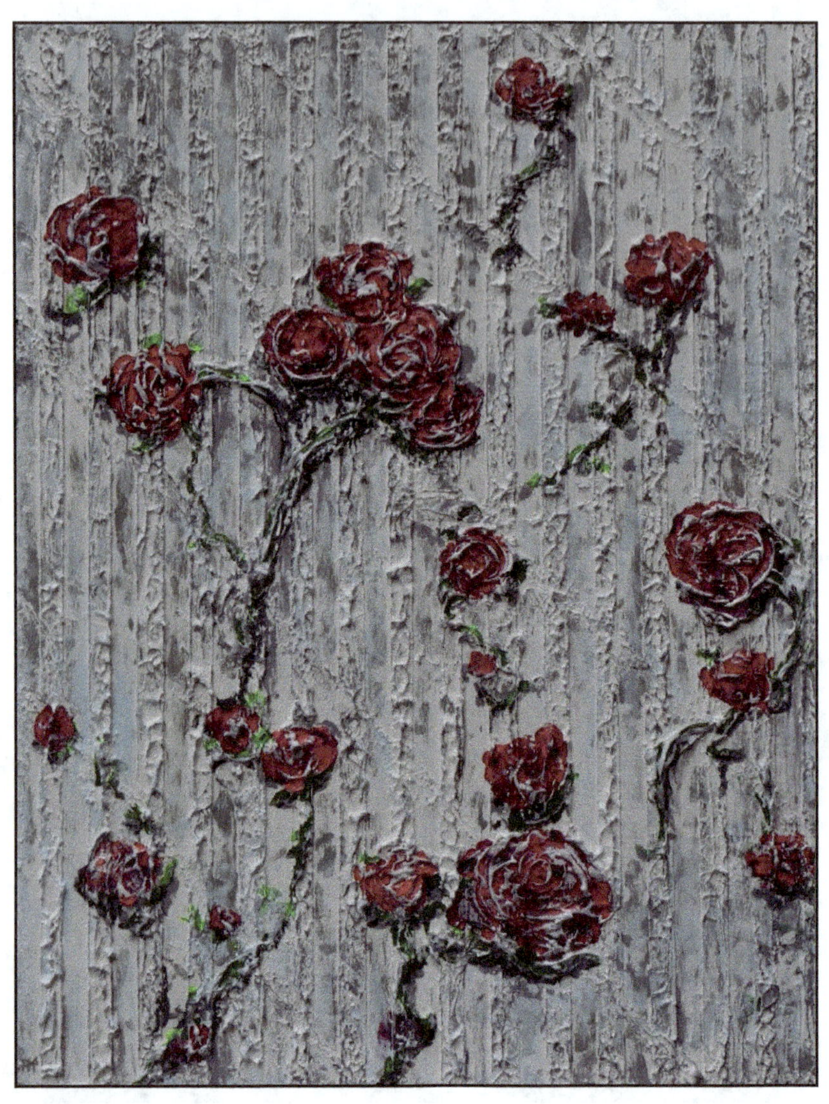

(Roses For) Remembrance

~ the fall will probably kill you ~
(from *Butch Cassidy and the Sundance Kid* 1969)

When the fall doesn't kill you,
it knocks you flat;
flat out of breath,
flat out of life,

all five senses dead,
only the sixth one remains.

Into that void
they come to you,
unbidden yet welcome;

ghosts and guilts,
burning-raw wounds,
as if filled with self-rubbing salt,
and fresh.

Time dries up,
becoming an alchemy
of memories and pain;

you can't gasp or cry
yet feel the cosmic cry
gasping: *please please forgive.*

Prison-bars for guilt,
for every little thing
you wish you could
do differently,
say differently,
but Time, dried up,
is gone.

Shadows for ghosts,
gray the ones who betrayed you,
blue the ones who carried you;
they slide in, across, and through: beloved.

You breathe again,
you see them dancing.

Your ghosts and guilts,
calling you to join them,

but the fall didn't kill you,
so you wash away the salt.

Always you see,
always you taste,
always you hear,
always you smell,
always you touch,
always you feel them within,

and always
you carry
roses for remembrance.

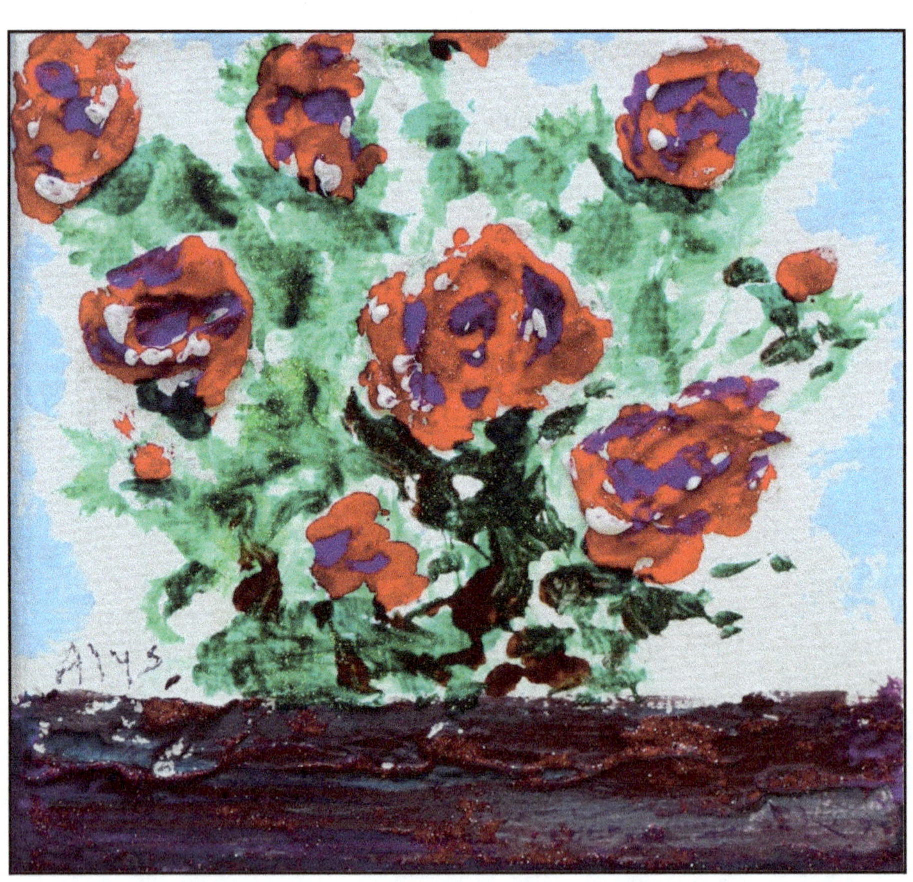

Paradise

(after *Paradise Lost* by John Milton)

What could be more sweet, what **better,**
than hearing your voice whisper **to**
me during the darkest night's **reign?**
When full sorrow has taken me **in,**
when the only light is the fire of **Hell,**
when I cannot breathe in or out, **than**
you come with a whisper to **serve**
salvation to my soul, whisking me away **in**
your golden embrace: my Paradise, my **Heav'n.**

You Hold My Heart

ever gentle, you hold my heart
as if it is the most fragile thing
the earth has ever seen

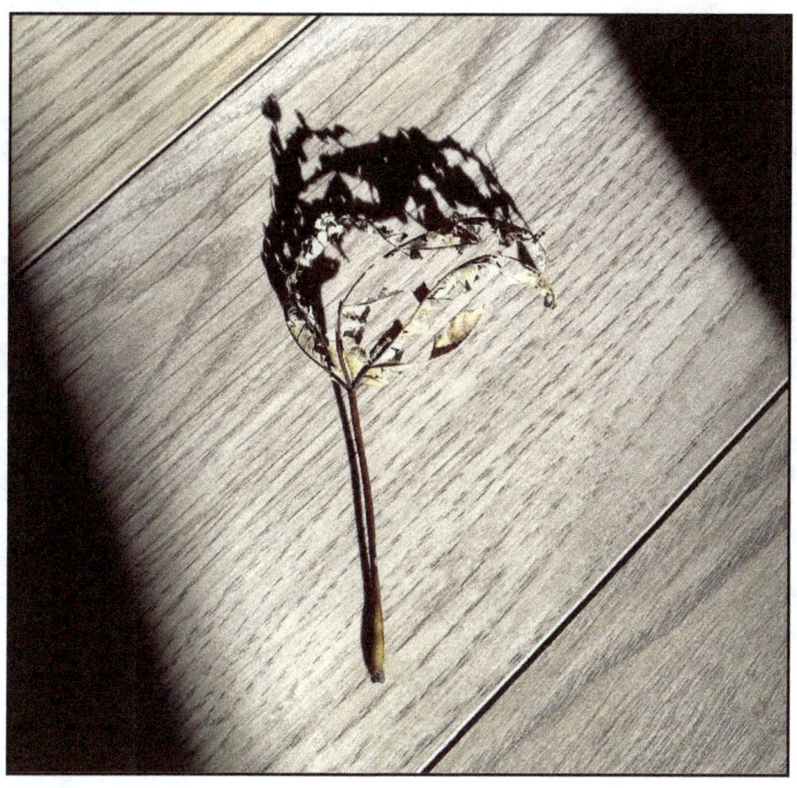

Axe-throwing haiku

Winter's last gasping
takes a toll upon my soul
our axes await

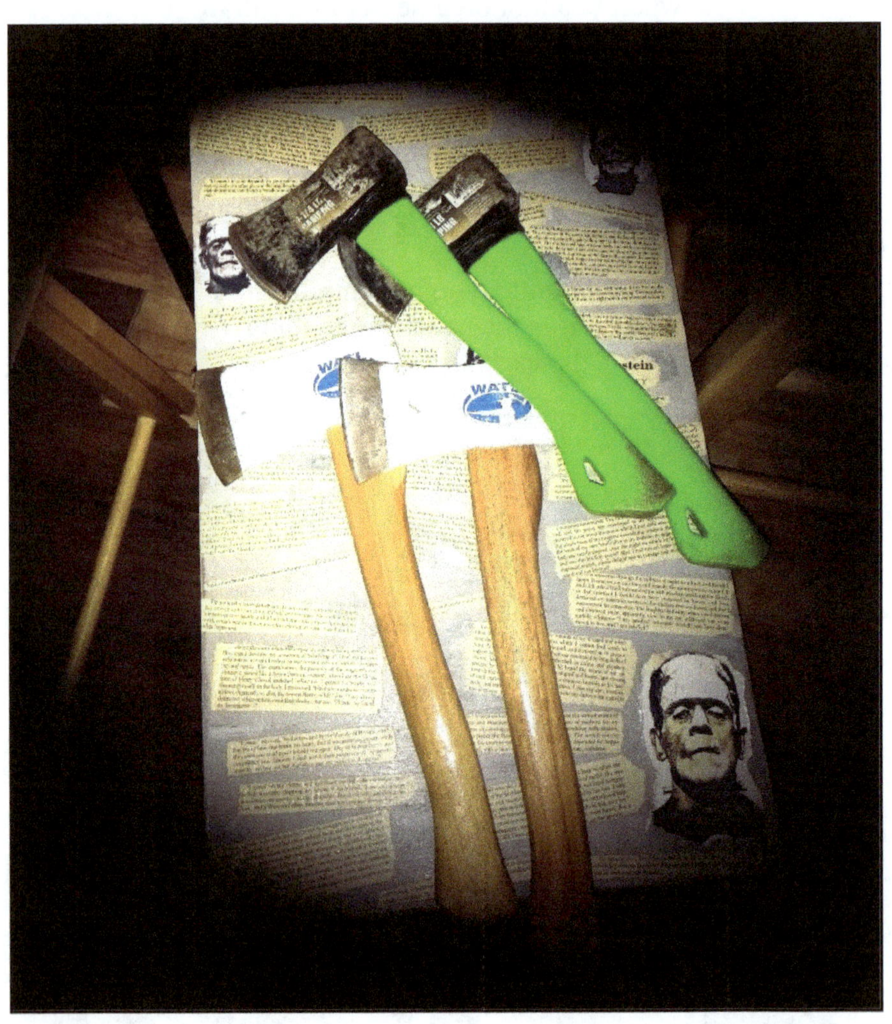

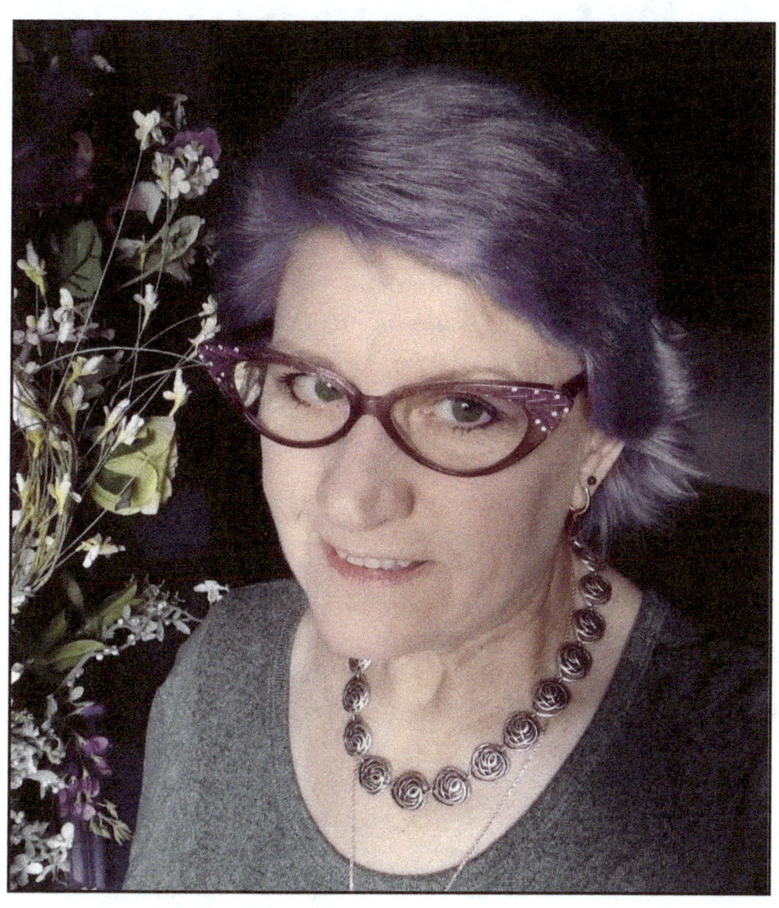

Alys Purple Hair

(Here's my personal and almost-completely-fictitious take on the great Roger Miller's classic song, *Kansas City Star*.)

Got a email just this morning
it was sent from NYC
it was typed and neatly written
offering me free studio space
and an agent to promote me
and sell all my abstract art
but I'm well-known here locally
I can't move; I'm a star

I go 'round my town
with my hair askew
and a-flying here and there
my flannels shirts
are paint-bespeckled
and my glasses match my hair

I'm the number one attraction
In the Walmart parking lot
I'm known as Alys Purple Hair
No thanks New York, thanks a lot

Alys Purple Haaaaaahhrrr
that's what I aaaaaare
yoodle-oooh-delady
you ought to see my car
I drive an old minivan with duct-taped sides
and a panther on the hood
I got a table down at Copper Still
yeah, my life here's purty good

I'm the number one attraction
In the Walmart parking lot
I'm known as Alys Purple Hair
So no thanks New York, thanks a lot

Alys Purple Haaaaaahhrrr
that's what I aaaaaare
yoodle-oooh-delady
you ought to see my car
I drive an old minivan with duct-taped sides
and a panther on the hood
I got a table down at Copper Still
yeah, my life here's purty good

I'm the number one attraction
In the Walmart parking lot
I'm known as Alys Purple Hair
So no thanks New York, thanks a lot

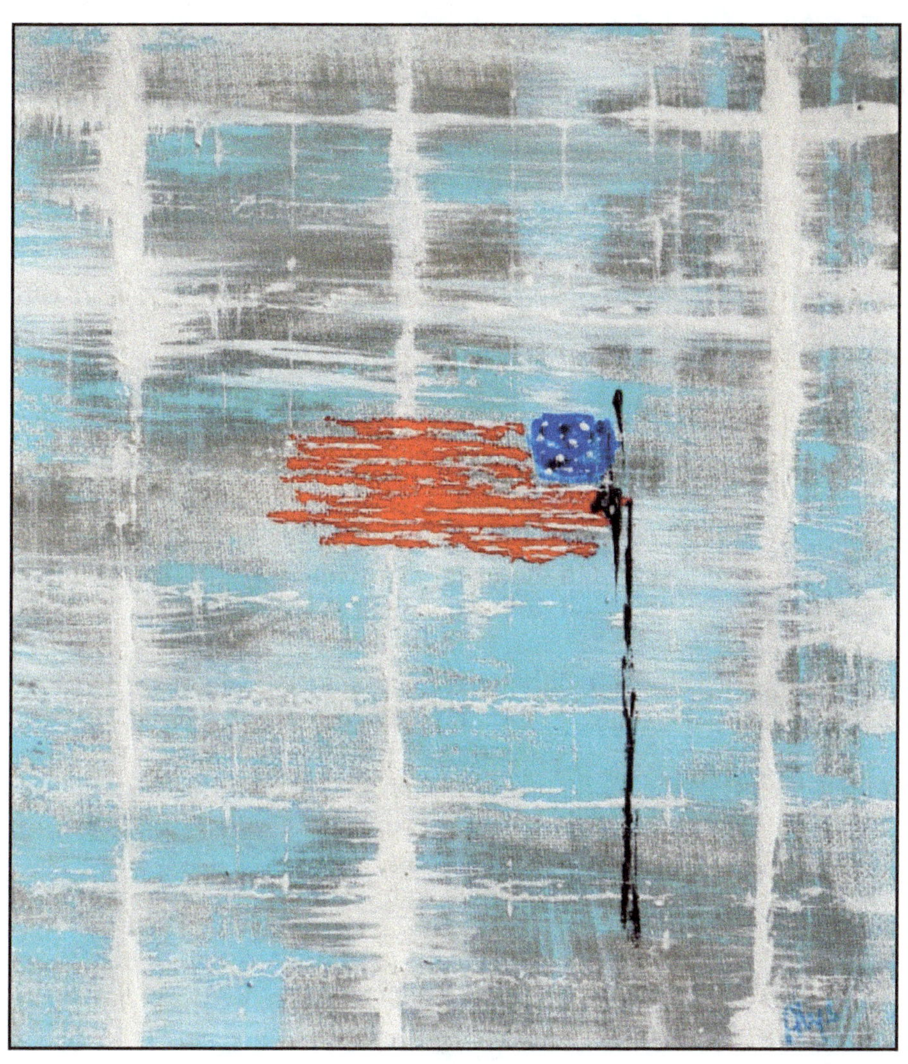

American Ode

Part One

Remember back
when you could say,
I am American and proud,
and it meant something
fierce and free,
to stand up.

America, I see you scream:
raw from love
and pain
and anger;
a C-section
a lobotomy
a knife's sharp plunge
and bullets fired,
fractious
shamed
made silent
by senseless
needless
hatred
and violence
and the weight of crime
and fervor for madness.

Remember your young girls?
On bicycles,
dreaming of love
and secret diaries,
their precious prophecies
calling back and forth
as they rode:
I'm gonna be a doctor!
I'm gonna be an astronaut!
I'm gonna be a teacher!
I'm gonna be President!

Those girls ~ ***your*** girls, America! ~
they were
trailed by bothersome
little brothers and sisters
tagging along behind,
in the dusk
their laughter
and their innocence,
echoes hollow
into today;
selfied, slouched, and surly

dreaming a foul dream
of over-sexualized narcissism,
no longer do they innocently ride,
instead they surf
searching seeking
eyes upon them
raking
rapacious
gotta get hits and shares and likes
parading
exposing
selling themselves
to a cacophony of invisible strangers
behind the screen;
undulations of abysmal abuse
are their only dream:
Look at ME!
LOOK at me!
LOOK AT ME!

Generations of battles
hard-won respect
and dreams of equality
crumble
with a twerk;

Remember your young boys?
With summer tans
playing outside and
making up the days
flying by like soaring eagles
in the bright blue sky,
building tree houses and forts,
playing baseball past sunset
'til they could not even see
that well-worn white ball,
they were Cowboys
and Indians
reliving a whitewashed past,
those innocent racists,
history was white

in their classrooms,
and their light sabers
flashed with dreams
of future glory:
I'm gonna be a doctor!
I'm gonna be an astronaut!
I'm gonna be a teacher!
I'm gonna be President!

Those boys ~ ***your*** boys, America! ~
they were
dreams that died
into today;
murdered
by assault weapons in classrooms
and the addictive power
of leveling up
eyes glued
narrowed with hate
thumbs flashing
shoot
kill
rape
attack
today's boys
do not know how to play
do not know how to see;

Remember lemonade stands
on your corners?
Neighborhood kids
calling out to passersby,
they were
dreaming their dreams,
future Fortune 500s
Wall Street aces
dreaming of building mansions
and driving flash cars,
those corner kids
with bright eyes
and coins jingling

selling lemonade
with visions
of wealth and prosperity,
We're entrepreneurs!
We're gonna be rich!
We're gonna be RICH!

But their dreams faded
into the nightmare of today;
the neighborhood kids
stand aloof,
these kids ~ your kids, America! ~
they are
escaping into
nothingness,
feeding addictions
to enter
some strange non-haven
non-heaven
of syringes, powders, and pills
snorting
sniffing
smoking
shooting up
leveling up
into
nothingness,
their dreamless eyes
dull
yet sharp with criminal intent,
they stand on corners ~ your corners, America! ~
your little consumers
of death;
do *they* believe
they're living your American dream?
(We're entrepreneurs!
We're gonna be rich!
We're gonna be RICH!)
but
they're just the first line
of offense

the introductory sales force
sell
sell
sell
the product
of flash lords
and drug cartels
and those kids ~ your kids, America! ~
have no dreams
as they die young
on the streets
or in jail
or in a room somewhere
alone.

Part Two

Remember your Founding Fathers
and the Mothers
silently beside them?
They stood up
and they dreamed
and created,
and sacrificed all
when you called to them
in their dreams;
they stood up
for freedom
from persecution,
for freedom
to believe,
for Faith separate from State,
and they *invented* it all for you;
the ideals,
a Great Experiment,
and they prayed privately
with sincere humility
to be led
by tolerance and righteousness,
and they governed publicly
for *The People*

with intent
and intentions
to create a more perfect Union,
and over time, America,
your sons and daughters
fought for you
died for you
died for ***you*** *god-damn-it*
for freedom
for rights
for humanity,
never perfect for all all of the time,
but they fought that good fight
over and over
and over,
sacrificing the blood of true believers,
that blue blood
is now colorless
and we have concentration camps
again
as we must *buy* this new America
because suddenly
you are for sale and we must buy
because we are patriotic
and if we say no then
we're commies who don't support the troops;

here, now, you are for sale
and mad men rule us
conglomerates poison us
monopolies rob us
religion suppresses us
corporations control us
lobbyists and television and headlines
create reality for us
as they master the puppets' strings,
and we race towards fascism
led by an orange-faced
self-*crown*'d
sneer
and the smarmy sanctimony

of so-called leaders
who believe
they are themselves
the voice of god and
holier than god and
good god by god
in god we trust
as presidential tweets
tweets
tweets
tweets
shame you and
bully us and
good god by god
could start World War Three
and they want our taxes to build a wall
as the Statue of Liberty weeps
(no more shall America proudly proclaim
give us your tired, your poor,
your huddled masses
yearning to breathe free!)
because children are in cages
torn from the arms of their parents

~ imagine the desperation of parents
to even start such a journey with their children
in tow knowing
their precious babies could die
drowned or starved or dehydrated
just trying to get ***here*** to you ~
and we won't even give toothpaste and soap
to the huddled masses
yearning to breathe free
let alone sanctuary
and a chance
at a better life
which our ancestors,
illegal immigrants all,
took
from the real Americans, Native Americans
and our Congress is a joke

without humor
without wit,
and our Supremes
fall low
failing you
failing us
failing all.

Part Three

Remember back when
we, *The People*,
your people
stood up
because we were taught
name-calling
is wrong and
The Golden Rule
is right,
and love thy neighbor
and Jesus loves us all
(*Jesus loves the little children
all the children of the world
red yellow black and white
they are precious in his sight
Jesus loves the little children of the world*)
and remember back when
we, *The People*,
your people
stood up and
sang out
Yes, Jesus loves me
(*for The Bible tells me so*)
and cried out *Hosanna*
fervent and sure
that God is good
thump
thump
thump
because The Bible tells me so
the path of righteousness is ours

thump
thump
thump
our great nation
birthed by Founding Mothers
and the Fathers,
who sowed the seeds,
as good Christians
filled with righteousness
and burning yearning
filled with God's love

yes, you were birthed
by them,
you were raised by them,
to offer hope,
to embrace freedoms,
of religion
of life
of liberty
and the pursuit of
happiness
to the world
to all
huddled masses yearning
to breathe free;

we *The People*
your people
faced and
embraced the world,
we cared
~ we *cared* ~
for others,
didn't we?

Part Four

Now
how
do we, *The People*,

your people,
fit
in this puzzle
that puzzles the world
and deceives the heart and soul,
how do we fit
in this puzzle
of *you*, America?

We, *The People*,
your people,
we rich
we poor
we homeless
we insane
we sick
we dying
we uninsured
(but sure
insurance companies
prosper),
we single mother
or father
we children
(starving
denied school lunches
because we cannot pay),
we subsidized
we hardworking
we unions
and non-unions
we workers
we families,
(watching the middle
disappear,
knowing our children
will not prosper,
we have only
desperation),
we are
all the colors

in the cultural spectrum
of human life
(yet we are
unrecognized
by the powers that be
who say
Corporations
are people);
we, *The People*,
your people,
we black
we white
we red
we yellow
we brown
we are
all the colors
in the genetic spectrum
of human skin
and eyes
and hair
and weight
and height
and shape;

we, *The People*,
your people,
we male
we female
we intersex
we transsex
we are
all the colors
in the genetic spectrum
of human sex;
we, *The People*,
your people,
we feminine
we masculine
we butch
we pansy

we two spirit
we gender queer
we cross dresser
we androgyne
we bitch
we pussy
(*grab 'em by the pussy*)
we colorful
are all colors
in the genetic spectrum
of human gender;
we, *The People*,
your people,
we homo
we hetero
we bi
we gay
we lesbian
we queer
we asex
we pan
we are
all the colors
in the genetic spectrum
of human sexuality

yes, we, *The People*,
your people,
are forsaken,
labeled and libeled
by those who claim
they speak
for god,
those god-damned
who *thump thump thump* that Bible
and point their fingers,
whose faces are red
with exertion and demand
and pomposity
and fervor
and self-righteous

tenacity,
who claim and exclaim
that they alone
know god
and what He wants,
the ones who claim
Jesus is their Savior
but they hate
in His name,
because (they say)
god demands their hate
for The Bible tells them so,
and now we bow
in silent fear
to the god-damned
as their greed consumes
and their lust betrays
and their power-hungry souls
take position
to rule.

Part Five

Yes, we, *The People*,
your people,
now second class
to the new first class
Corporate Personhood,
as our Government
(*for The People by The People*)
rapes us
with violence and apathy,
god-damned sanctimonious politicians
sound-bites us in the ass
and we blindly follow
and stupidly believe,
we are
led by Oscar-worthy
one-liners and platitudes
and an orange self-*crown*'d
~ *corona*'d ~

puppet
assaults us with
tweets
tweets
tweets
while sanctimony drips
from the obscene
condescending sneer
in the pasty self-righteousness
of yet another white-haired
old white man
a smiling True Believer
who truly believes
he and he alone
knows
the mind of god.

O God, America!

As you slip away
into Fascism
(*we fought **that** war*
*we died in **that** war*
*we won **that** war*
god-damn-it!)
as you slip away
one sneer at a time,
one tweet at a time
one *corona*'d death
one confirmation at a time
one Congressional resolution at a time
and our rights and progress
are stripped away
and we are left to die
as we are shoved
swirling
drowning in their
death cult
as our leaders lead us
strategically
down the garden-of-eden path

into a nightmare world
of hatred and fear,
but *WE THE PEOPLE*
are to blame
are we not?

Because we know
WE know
We KNOW
WE KNOW
it is all a lie.

We know
the rich old white men
the great and powerful Ozes
behind your curtains
are liars,
yes, we know,
yet we
willfully
will-lessly
we sit
sheltered
in stillness
corona'd
intravenously
osmosisly
fed
from boob-tube
and internet tube,
we tube-screwed
slack-jawed
true believers
we sit
and we say
we believe
and we cry
Hosanna
as we exhale the hatred
and we exhale the lies
of the god-damned

because their breath
became our breath
and their lies
became our truths
and their hate
became our hate,
and we gasp out
your death
with the lies
that doom you, America,
and we surrender the dream,
the Great Experiment,
because it is so much easier
to **sit**
and do nothing
and it is so much easier
to **sit**
and say nothing
and it is so much easier
to **sit**
and resist nothing
yes, it is so much easier
to **sit**
than to
stand up.

Can we *The People*
your people
remember
how to stand up?

Part Six

I am an American.

I'm water-boarded
gasping
grasping
stymied
corona'd
in a swamp

of melancholic despair.
Am I alone?
Am I *you*, America?

Are we still *We The People*,
your people?

We tweet
we twerk
we level up
we buy
we believe
we pray
we exhale
and America
screams
silently
into a void
of destruction
and death.
Who are we *The People* now?
~ the *corona*'d people ~
your people.

Did I survive?
Am I still
an American?

Part Seven

What are we now?

Are we still America?

~ we *The People* ~
of . . .

Did we stand up?

Driving

Sometimes
I feel like I could drive forever,
passing beyond
the rolling southern Indiana hills,

through memory-stabbing miles in Alabama
where history hangs sorrowfully,
an eternal fog of despair,

then Mississippi,
patched with red earth
that makes my heart ache,
for the blood spilled
and for my old home in Georgia
~ *always on my mind* ~

then down to where the tall pines grow
like sentinels
watching over this Dorian gray portrait
marred by evil,

then the tall pines merge
within the cradling arms of the Grandpa trees,

live oaks aged and wise
with branches caressing
earth and sky,
and mystic's drapings
of Spanish Moss swaying
~ *beckoning* ~

then,
then I am home.

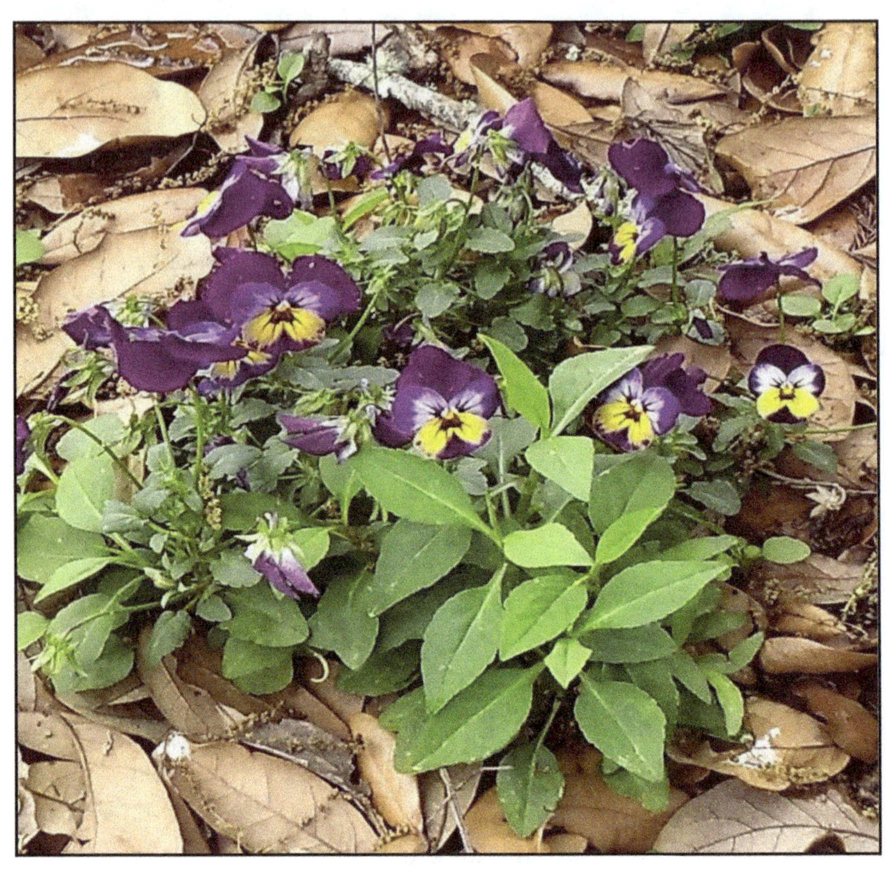

Sea Legs

Like a sailor back to port
I find my sea legs
don't work on land;

I focus on minutiae at my feet,
just-birthed Spring flowers
draw my eyes
from a tilting horizon,
their sweet faces smile up at me
they salute me buoyantly
from the tilting earth,
these old friends and new;

still wobbling,
I must smile back,
their colors are
infectious with joy,

and then when
I finally look up again

I see my dearest Spanish Moss,
gently singing on a southern breeze,

welcoming me
home from sea.

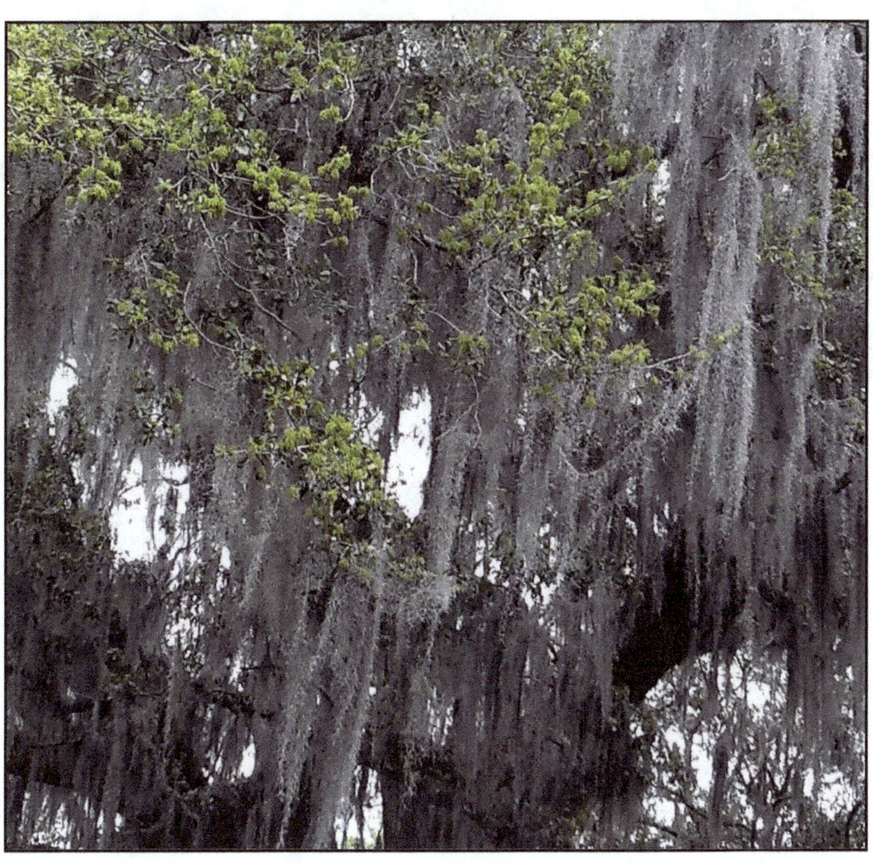

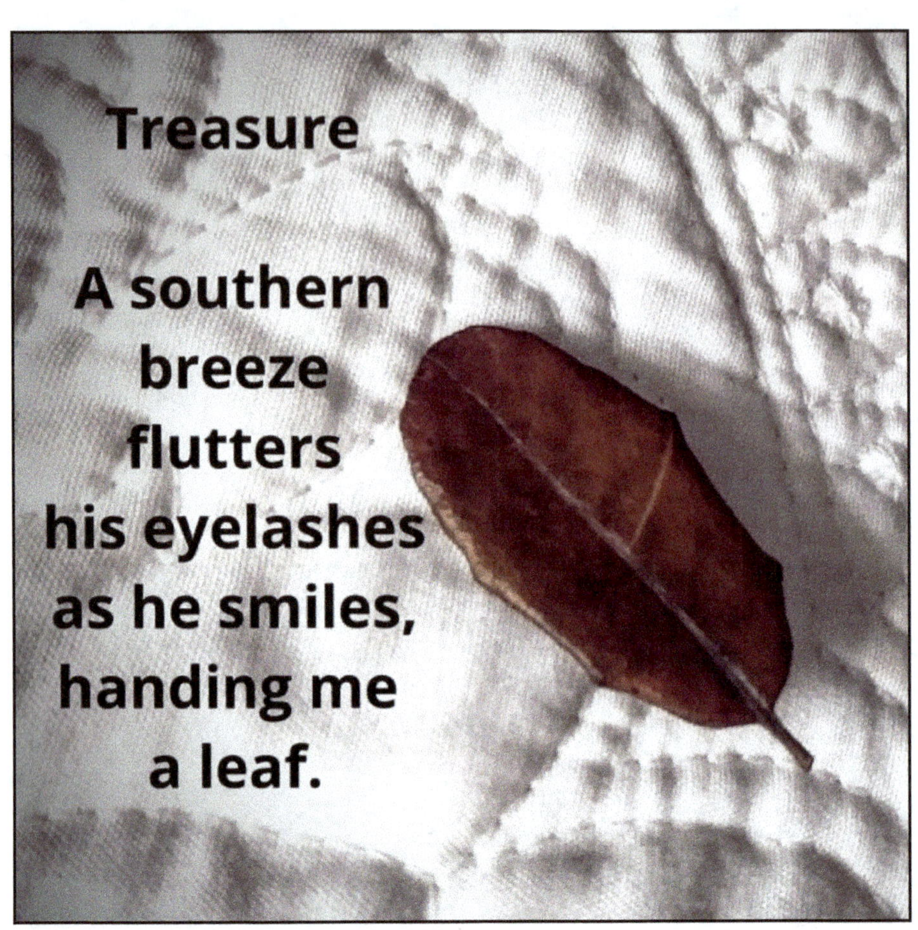

Instapoem V Treasure

About the Author

Alys Caviness-Gober is an anthropologist, artist, and writer. Despite lifelong disabilities, Alys perseveres with art and nonprofit volunteering. She comes late to the life of a professional artist; after receiving her MA in Anthropology, Alys taught Anthropology and Women's Studies and was a PhD candidate in Applied Linguistics until her disabilities worsened.

Alys serves on the Noblesville Cultural Arts Council and is active in the local arts scene. In 2011, she started selling artwork online and locally as *Creative Expressions Arts*, and was juried into the *Hamilton County Artists' Association* in both photography (2012) and 2D categories (2013). She is the co-founder of *NICE* (*Noblesville Interdisciplinary Creativity Expo*); in 2018 NICE received an Indiana Humanities project grant.

In November of 2014, she founded an all-volunteer 501(c)(3) Arts organization, *Community • Education • Arts, Inc.* (CEArts), providing the community with diverse arts projects and programming. CEArts hosts annual two place-making projects, *The Polk Street Review* (TPSR) and *Noblesville Interdisciplinary Creativity Expo* (NICE), and diverse digital content, including online *Arts Showcase* exhibit opportunities for writers and artists, and @theroundtable podcast and short videos series. Alys is editor of the annual TPSR anthology, recipient of three Indiana Arts Commission grants (2018, 2019, 2020).

Alys is a FY2017 Indiana Arts Commission *Individual Artist Project* Grant Award recipient, for which she created a series of paintings expressing life with hidden disabilities. She was selected for *IUPUI Arts and Humanities Institute's Religion Spirituality, and the Arts* 2018/19 seminar, is a film reviewer for *Midwest Film Journal*, and has been an invited presenter at *Poetry Society of Indiana* conferences and Monicat Data's arts and technology 2019 *Yellow Summit*. Alys' artwork and poetry have received national and international recognition.

www.ingramcontent.com/pod-product-compliance
Lightning Source LLC
LaVergne TN
LVHW010608110826
845149LV00003B/817

* 9 7 8 0 9 9 9 8 8 5 8 4 0 *